KOREAN FURNITURE

KOREAN

Edward Reynolds Wright   Man Sill Pai

FURNITURE

Elegance and Tradition

KODANSHA INTERNATIONAL LTD.
Tokyo, New York and San Francisco

PHOTO CREDITS

Kenji Miura: Plates 1–5, 8–16, 18–25, 27–42, 44, 47, 50–54, 56, 57, 59–65, 67, 69–79, 83, 84, 86–92, 98, 100–109, 117, 118, 125, 127, 131–139, 143, 146, 148, 149–152; pages 2, 3, 5, 6, 142, 182

George Mitchell: Plates 6, 7, 17, 26, 43, 55, 93, 110, 113–115, 128, 145, 147; pages 7, 12, 136–141, 152

Distributed in the United States by Kodansha International/ USA Ltd., through Harper & Row, Publishers, Inc., 10 East 53rd Street, New York, New York 10022.

Published by Kodansha International Ltd., 12–21, Otowa 2-chome, Bunkyo-ku, Tokyo 112 and Kodansha International/USA Ltd., with offices at 10 East 53rd Street, New York, New York 10022 and The Hearst Building, 5 Third Street, Suite 430, San Francisco, California, 94103.

Printed in Japan.
First edition, 1984

LCC 83–48878
ISBN 0–87011–652–5
ISBN 4–7700–1152–0 (in Japan)

Library of Congress Cataloging in Publication Data

Wright, Edward Reynolds.
    Korean furniture.

    Includes bibliographical references and index.
    1. Furniture—Korea.   I. Pai, Man Sill. II. Title.
NK2673.6.W75 1984   749.29519   83–48878
ISBN 0–87011–652–5 (U.S.)

CONTENTS

THE DECADES OF THE 1960s and 1970s saw a great surge of interest in the study and collection of Korean furniture. As a result, knowledge about shapes, styles, proportions, joinery, woods, and provenance has been broadened and is still increasing. There are recent works in these areas in Korean by Man Sill Pai of Ewha Womans University, Park Young-kyu of the staff of the National Museum of Korea, and Sunu Choi, Director of the National Museum of Korea. Some university museums, including those at Ewha Womans University and Koryŏ (Korea) University in Seoul, have undertaken studies of their substantial collections of Korean furniture. One suspects, however, that much more information is available than scholars have thus far been able to research, catalogue, and record. One of the problems is in trying to pull together information and opinion from quite diverse sources, including scholars, private collectors, museums, dealers, contemporary cabinetmakers, and the last generation of Koreans who actually used the furniture (in general, those fifty years old or more). Some gaps in knowledge will be filled by this book; at the same time, the authors acknowledge that more study and exploration is needed. Knowledge of the areas mentioned above can stand refinement, and there are other areas about which little has been written and in which substantial research is necessary.

For example, more exacting historical analysis is needed. Were styles of furniture of the middle and late nineteenth century of a more or less similar appearance to those before the seventeenth century? What evolution in furniture styles and function took place over the initial three centuries of the Yi dynasty (the fifteenth through seventeenth centuries)? Did commoners in those times use different types of furniture for specialized functions, or did they just store clothing and other possessions in simple boxes, or what? Perhaps historians have the information and tools to further explore and answer these kinds of questions.

Another area open to further study concerns lacquering techniques. Most Yi dynasty furniture was rubbed with oil, and the process is generally known and agreed

9

PREFACE

upon. Lacquering in Korea, however, was not common, so coherent knowledge of the art is spotty. It would fill a significant gap if someone undertook the task of bringing some consistency to the bits and pieces of knowledge and opinion about lacquering techniques in Yi dynasty Korea.

With regard to traditional symbolism, it would be good if someone would do a systematic survey before "modernity" completely takes over—especially in the countryside—to try to discern the extent to which people associate symbolic meanings with particular design motifs. In the context of this book, such a survey would relate to forms seen in the metalwork and decoration on furniture. It is not at all unusual to encounter different ideas about such symbols; it would be an important contribution if clarity could be brought to their perceived meanings.

Despite these gaps in knowledge, much of the information in this volume will be new to many readers—especially those from an English-speaking audience. The drawings and photographs portray a variety of types and styles that should aid the reader not only to understand the similarities and differences among them, but also to gain an appreciation for the "look" of traditional Korean furniture in comparison with that of China and Japan. Drawings of construction techniques constitute an important portion of the book and should clearly illustrate that the "simple" appearance of Korean furniture is misleading—the hidden, underlying structure is quite complex; the craftsman surely worked very hard to convey a superficial impression of simplicity, while successfully concealing or downplaying the sophisticated construction techniques. One section relates furniture to the traditional Korean life-style, while others discuss woods and finishes used in cabinetry and metal fittings and their functions and shapes. It is the hope of the authors that this volume will provide a helpful and informative introduction to the subject and a stimulus to more widespread interest, study, and research.

In this kind of project, the division of labor between or among authors and editors is seldom clear. In general, however, it can be pointed out that the superb drawings and sketches of furniture, construction, and detail were provided by Man Sill

Pai, while the final text of the book in its English rendering was the responsibility of Edward Wright, who assumes full responsibility for all textual shortcomings. Photographs in Korea were taken by George Mitchell and the Yang Jŏng-Hae studio, and those in the United States and Japan by Kenji Miura.

Wright wishes to express his genuine appreciation and indebtedness to his co-author and many, many others (they know who they are!) for his gradual enlightenment—however incomplete—on the subject of this book. It has been in process for eight years. He especially wishes to mention his mother, Eunice L. Wright, who shares his affinity for the arts and crafts of Korea; her encouragement and support have always been instrumental and deeply appreciated. Kim Schuefftan, editor at Kodansha International, has coaxed, encouraged, and contributed in a multitude of ways to render the text more readable and to make the book considerably bigger than originally intended. Kodansha's interest in and support of this project are gratefully acknowledged.

Kyoto and Seoul
February, 1984

Astartling realization that came while this book was being written is that not many nations or peoples of the world have a long tradition of making furniture. Further, even fewer have furniture traditions that have remained relatively unchanged for centuries.

The furniture of Korea is practically unique among the furnitures of the world: it is part of a tradition that goes back well over a millennium, and furniture designs have remained relatively unchanged from at least the seventeenth century. This monolithic tradition, immediately recognizable as Korean, was "discovered" by the West in the late 1940s and 1950s. Since then, what has captured the attention and recognition of the world is that Korean furniture is elegant, robust, and combines simplicity with beauty.

Korea's cultural and artistic debt to China is substantial; even so, Korea's cabinetry tradition is unique due in part to the insular and conservative nature of the society—until recent years Korea was known as the "Hermit Kingdom." Furniture forms changed little after the seventeenth century, and some types originated long before then. The Koguryŏ dynasty (37 B.C.–A.D. 668) Dancing Figures tomb on the Yalu River, dating to the fourth or fifth century, has wall paintings showing a bed platform and small serving table not unlike some in use during the nineteenth century. Excavations from the Three Kingdoms period have uncovered lacquered woodwork in tombs of the Paekche (18 B.C.–A.D. 660) and Pre-Unified Silla (57 B.C.–A.D. 668) kingdoms. From the period after Silla unified the peninsula (668–938) there is an intact ninth century musical instrument preserved in the Shōsō-in repository in Nara, Japan. This twelve-stringed *kayagŭm* (a "zither") is artfully shaped of paulownia wood and closely resembles its present-day counterpart. A great deal of lacquered woodwork was produced on the Korean peninsula during the Koryŏ dynasty (938–1392), and a few pieces are extant. A highly decorated tenth-century Koryŏ box is housed in the Hōryū-ji temple, also in Nara, Japan. Other Koryŏ boxes have intricate

13

INTRODUCTION

mother-of-pearl inlay. It is notable that such boxes have proportions and shapes similar to document, incidentals, and wedding boxes made throughout the Yi dynasty (1392–1911) and up to the present.

The most concrete evidence of continuity of shapes and forms of Korean furniture over the past two centuries (at least) is a delightful genre painting by Sin Yun-bok (b. 1758). This interior scene of a traditional village drinking house makes it clear that furniture styles and customs have changed not at all from the artist's time to the twentieth century. Almost the identical scene can be viewed, with minor modifications, in the remote Korean countryside today; and as recently as the 1960s, it was not unusual almost anywhere in the country.

In Korea's neighboring country, Japan, the seventeenth century also saw the emergence of the typical form of Japanese furniture—the chest of drawers. This type of chest evolved together with the kimono and developed mainly as storage for this garment.

As in Japan, the primary type of Korean furniture is the chest. Shelves, tables, trays, desks, beds, and small boxes were made, but chests of various kinds are preeminent. In contrast to the Japanese drawered chest, Korean chests are little more than large boxes—they are mostly empty inside. Drawers, when present, are small. In general the Korean chest has simple, straight lines. Curves do appear, however, on the legs of chests and desks (Plates 5, 6, 26) and on the winglike ends of some desks and book storage cabinets (Plates 25, 26, 152). The Koreans had a strong feeling for wood and for wood grain patterns and used a rather limited range of woods in vigorous and decorative ways. Most often, wood with an attractive grain was split into panels, which were used in a balanced, mirror-image composition on the front of a chest (see Plates 11, 33). Iron metalwork is functional or decorative or both, while most brass metalwork is largely decorative.

There are three basic chest forms: the simple box (Plate 2); the two-unit stacked chest (essentially two boxes; Plate 8); and the chest with two or three (rarely more) levels of compartments within a frame (Plate 5).

Clothing and kitchen chests were always placed against a wall. Therefore careful attention was paid to the appearance of the front, relatively little to the sides, and none to the back. The front was artfully designed, often displaying the matching wood panels described above and complementary metal fittings of brass or iron.

Coffers and boxes of varying shapes and designs were used for coins, clothing, wedding mementos, documents, stationery, women's makeup and incidentals, and painting and writing materials, among others. These were not placed against a wall, so finished work appears on the sides and back as well as on the front. Though chest forms in general were dictated by tradition and usage, size and appearance depended on the space and placement within the household, the woods available, and the individual craftsman's impulse.

Since the early 1970s there has been a dramatic surge in interest in the furniture of the Yi dynasty among Koreans themselves. Probably it is at least partially because of the drain of traditional objects from Korea into Japan and the West that the Korean public became interested in the collection and preservation of objects that only a' short while before had been taken for granted or thrown out as junk. During the seventies, city dwellers who made trips to the countryside to try and salvage family furniture relegated to barns and storage sheds often found the furniture gone, most having been bought up by antique dealers based in the big cities. Many of these dealers established their own workshops for restoring furniture that in most instances had seen the ravages of the elements. Pieces that have been preserved in good condition for a century or more are rare. With the dearth of original pieces, reproductions— both carefully and hastily made ones—have become popular, particularly ones made with wood salvaged from older pieces in extreme disrepair.

Though concern for cultural preservation has always been strong among dedicated Korean scholars, museum curators, and serious collectors, such people were a very small group and without wide influence. Yet Korea has its own tradition of collecting and preserving art and artifacts. There is evidence that, at least through the Yi dynasty and probably before, royalty and the aristocracy maintained private collections of art and craft objects, mostly Korean, but occasionally Chinese. Many Buddhist temple treasures also were protected and passed down through the centuries, particularly works in bronze.

With the Japanese annexation of Korea in 1910, Japanese collectors gained direct access to Korean cultural assets, thereby dramatically enlarging the collecting population and eventually resulting in much Korean art being sent to Japan. Many Japanese and Korean scholars have been of the opinion that collecting of and scholarship on Korean art have been largely products of this Japanese exposure and interest. A guide to Korean studies published in 1980 reflects this attitude: "The Japanese were the first to start collecting and studying Korean art in the early years of the twentieth century, and most of the preliminary works were written in Japanese."[1] The Japanese, principally through studying and classifying, undoubtedly broadened and popularized interest in Korean arts and crafts in the twentieth century. The same process happened in Japan as well, with Western interest and scholarship often pointing the way for Japanese activity in art and craft.

The intensity of the Japanese interest, however, stimulated some wealthy Koreans to competitively collect art and antiquities. The first prominent twentieth century Korean collector is generally considered to have been the late Chun Hyung-pil, whose impressive and vast collection is periodically on view at the small Kansong Museum in Seoul. Because of the limited display space, only a minute portion of the collection can be put on exhibit at any time. Two other prominent collectors are Lee Byung-chul, whose private museum is located in Yong-In, south of Seoul, and the late Lee Hong-gun, whose nearly five thousand-piece collection was taken over in 1981 by the National Museum of Korea. Lee Hong-gun is said to have concluded that, under the Japanese occupation (1910–45), an effective way to maintain and transmit the national spirit of the Korean people was to collect and help preserve Korean cultural treasures. His collection was exhibited in the private Kongwŏn Art Museum in Seoul from 1967 until Lee's death in 1980. Another Korean, Yi In-yong, compiled a vast and valuable library of Yi dynasty books and manuscripts, "inspired" by

Japanese collectors who were combing the country for rare volumes.

The Korean War (1950–53) had a devastating effect on many private collections because of physical destruction and social chaos. To cite one case, a collection of rare Yi dynasty books housed at Ewha Womans University in Seoul was totally destroyed during the fighting. In a happier vein, Kim Chewon, then director of the Korean National Museum, personally supervised the transport of many of the museum's treasures from Seoul south to Pusan, saving them from destruction or from being carried to the communist north. After the war, in a time of widespread economic deprivation, many valuable art objects made their way to the marketplace and were sold at quite low prices in the 1950s and 1960s. Also after the war, many rare books were torn apart by unknowing antique dealers for lining traditional furniture and reproductions thereof to give an appearance of antiquity.

Especially since the Korean War, an increasing number of Westerners has become attracted to old Korean furniture and to reproductions and designs based on traditional Korean models. Possibly the reason for this attraction is that traditional Korean furniture blends well with a very wide range of interior styles and decors. Korean furniture in general has a quietness and dignity that does not blatantly call attention to itself but rather fits into most interiors with grace and ease. It seems as at home in a "mixed" contemporary setting as in traditional surroundings. Lines are either horizontal or vertical, displaying few of the curves and eccentricities found in European furniture. The furniture has a low center of gravity, as it were, a stability. Pieces can be whimsical (Plate 12) as well as sober (Plate 2). This unselfconscious simplicity of line is seen equally in rough-hewn country pieces (Plate 33) and in royal household furniture (Plate 27). Even pieces decorated with carving, lacquer, or inlay of mother-of-pearl retain a total impression of purity of line and proportion. This "classic" purity of proportion is clearly illustrated when small pieces are photographed: often, if no indication of size is present, they are easily mistaken for very large pieces (Plate 147). Most Yi dynasty furniture extant is from the nineteenth and early twentieth centuries, though some eighteenth and, rarely, seventeenth century pieces are also to be found.

One Korean scholar has written that the salient feature of traditional Korean craftsmanship can be said to be "the attempt to reduce artifice to a minimum with the intention of making the most of the materials used—such as the texture of stone or the grain of wood—so as to achieve in a manner of speaking an incomplete, an imperfect perfection."[2] This is in keeping with the views of the late Muneyoshi (Sōetsu) Yanagi of Japan, who has referred to Korean crafts in terms of "an unmeditated beauty," created by nature with borrowed human hands. Yanagi's comments on pottery can be applied equally to woodwork: "They [Korean craftsmen] live in a world where accuracy and inaccuracy are met, yet differentiated. This state of mind is the very foundation from which the beauty of the Korean pot flows."[3] Japanese collectors tend to prize Korean crafts for these characteristics, and Yanagi is generally considered to have played a pioneering and major role in focusing on and helping to articulate the nature and attributes of Korean folk arts and crafts.

The products of Korean Yi dynasty furniture makers were in harmony with the traditional rooms with their low ceilings and heated (*ondol*), paper-covered floors. One cataloguer has described this relationship in these terms: "Yi woodcraft rejects unnecessary lines and decoration in order to substantiate the inner quality and the result is a daring simplicity" with ample unornamented space "and well-planned proportion. The proportion applies not only to lines and planes of . . . furniture but also to the overall space of a room, and the unique linear and dimensional harmony within and without. . . ."[4]

The "Koreanness" of Korean crafts is a quality or a group of qualities that resists easy formulation, yet this is something that deserves serious consideration. Though certain aspects of design, structure, and technique relate to neighboring traditions in China and Japan, an essential, unique, Korean quality certainly exists. This may be abstracted in terms of four interrelated characteristics; these are somewhat intangible, subtle qualities, more in the order of impressions or flavors, and do not necessarily relate directly to the design, form, and art traditions of the country.

1. While the traditional Korean craftsman certainly achieved balance and harmony

of design, his efforts in general do not show the preoccupation with formal perfection and highly refined technical virtuosity that is found to a far greater extent in both Japan and China.

2. This is not to say that Korean things are all crude. Some are, while others are detailed and refined. Yet they all seem to project a "sense" of materials, a feeling that the craftsman has allowed his materials just to be themselves. In furniture, individual woods are respected for what they are and are used or allowed or aided to show their own characteristics and personalities. The woodworker's sense of materials seems almost playful at times; at other times, the effects obtained are spectacular or majestic.

3. Because the Korean craftsman does not force his materials to perform tricks or to be obscured by obvious technique, but, rather, lets his work flow with the character and idiosyncracies of the materials, no two pieces of Korean furniture seem to be quite the same. Despite the fact that the craftsman has "let go," in a sense, his presence behind and as a part of the process is strongly felt. Korean objects, furniture especially, somehow transmit something directly from craftsman to user. This sense of innocent, artless directness is part of their great appeal.

4. Finally, the Korean craftsman seems more involved with the whole object than with the parts—details or decoration—of which it is fashioned. In furniture, detailed work sometimes appears in metal fittings, carving, mother-of-pearl inlay, and painted ox horn. Yet somehow such detail, no matter how impressive, takes a secondary place beside the form that it complements and embellishes.

To properly understand Yi dynasty furniture styles and usages, it is important to know something of the period's social and cultural underpinnings. The dominant class-consciousness and hierarchical socio-political structure of the Yi centuries was based upon the Neo-Confucian model, which drew from various sources, including Taoism and Buddhism. Yi dynasty society viewed the universe as hierarchical and regarded social and interpersonal relations as greatly circumscribed, especially between members of different classes and status groups, between elder and younger, and between man and woman. Each level of society from the ruler on down was expected to act in certain ways. In effect, the system was quite conservative, and the highly structured Neo-Confucianism of the dynasty encouraged rather rigid social patterns and distinctions to evolve.

Outside of the royal family, there were two clearly defined classes in traditional Korean society as well as the status groups. At the peak were the *yangban*, officials and descendants of high-ranking officials, who formed a landed aristocracy. Mostly resident in provincial cities or the capital city, they were among other things absentee landlords who lived mostly on rent from tenant farmers. Most participated in some way in local or national politics. The second class level in Yi Korea included the *sang-in*, the merchant class, and the *kong-in* or artisans, including wood craftsmen. The two had comparable status. Upward mobility, especially for the *sang-in*, was possible by attaining government position through the open Imperial Examination system; however, few could succeed, since the examination was oriented toward the background and preparation of the *yangban*. In the Yi dynasty, the *sang-in* and *kong-in* were often grouped together and referred to as *kong-sang-in*, especially for government taxation purposes.

The *chung-in*, "intermediary people," has been identified as a special status group in Yi society. They were the offspring of marriages between *yangban* and *kong-sang-in*. The *chung-in* males often filled clerical and minor roles in the government—roles usually passed on to their sons. *Chung-in* were generally looked down upon by both *yangban* and *kong-sang-in* because of their interclass origins.

The lowest Yi dynasty status group, more accurately perceived perhaps in terms of caste, was the *chŏn-in*, or "low-born people." This included servants, Buddhist monks, prostitutes, shaman priests or priestesses, farm serfs, and butchers. Members of the *chŏn-in* were looked down upon and had no normal entree into social channels accessible to the two established classes or to the *chung-in*. They could not enter their names in the national register, nor were they accepted for military service.[5]

It can be concluded that the conservative and orthodox Neo-Confucianism of the time encouraged and helped the Korean nation to turn inward and develop a social structure and a life-style that were efficacious in sustaining an uninterrupted 518 years of rule by the Yi family. Strong Chinese influences were received without great trouble, for the Koreans had long accepted elements of Chinese tradition as their own.

It is noteworthy that not only the Yi dynasty's Neo-Confucian superstructure but also the deeply rooted shamanism and Buddhism tend to persist in the social patterns of contemporary Korea, along with the more recently added Christianity. This has been observed in the field research of a number of scholars in recent years, particularly anthropologists. One Western scholar of Korean folk culture has described this mixture well, and her observations are worth reiterating to substantiate the case for continuity in the Korean cultural tradition and in the symbolism and motifs used in traditional Korean art forms, including furniture and its metalwork:

> Buddhism . . . has been practiced on the peninsula since the fourth century, but it has taken on a particularly Korean tint, having for centuries coexisted with other belief systems, sometimes less than amicably, and having through the years absorbed elements of shamanistic belief and Confucian rites. Any visitor to a Buddhist temple, for example, might notice an abundance of shoes outside a tiny tile-roofed shrine, a sign that inside on the glossy wooden floor are people making offerings of prayer, incense, or rice and fruit. . . . This popular shrine is dedicated to the mountain spirit depicted in paintings of an old man and a tiger and indeed, a painting of this spirit from the shamanistic pantheon appears on the wall behind the altar. Furthermore, many temples regularly hold a kind of *chesa*, a rite for ancestors, a ritual with a particularly Confucian flavor, both on anniversaries of the deaths of family members remembered by the living and on one day each month for those who died on unknown occasions. One Christian woman, who privately arranged for a Buddhist temple to perform a *chesa* for her deceased father because a shaman

had divined this unfeasted spirit as the cause of her family troubles, explained ... that "even Catholics have ancestors." At the same time, shamans themselves, who are mainly women and who attract a high proportion of women followers, also perform remedial rituals addressing household problems created by unremembered ancestors, including those on the maternal as well as the paternal side. Statues of Buddha and paintings of Buddhist nuns often grace shamans' altars, and shamans sometimes consult a one year's almanac or utilize some esoteric principle of ultimately Taoist origins with the same facility as horoscope readers, though the latter usually work more closely with the classical Chinese *Book of Changes* which contains essential tenets of Taoism. Confucian rituals, all restricted to men and some traditionally limited to high officials of the court, seem to have incorporated less from shamanism and Buddhism than the reverse, and their strict principles in effect still seem to serve as a model of decorum and moderation from which Buddhism and shamanism offer an expressive release. . . . Except for Christians . . . most Koreans do not identify themselves as members of any one organized religion. Spiritual life is a melange of religious strains which is sometimes evidenced in formal or contemplative acts, sometimes as members of any one organized religion.

Amidst the ethic of hard work, economic struggle, and moderation visible in Seoul, there is the occasional sound of a shaman's clanging cymbals or a monk's wooden clapper and the flash of golden bowls of fruit at Buddhist, shamanistic, and Confucian altars. The quiet concentration of a sunrise offering at a shrine and the revelry of a midnight lantern parade on Buddha's Birthday each break the routines of daily life.[6]

This age-old but still vital social, cultural and religious melange provides the foundation for an identifiably Korean life-style, one aspect of which has been its rich and distinctive furniture tradition. The relationship between the Yi dynasty's life-style and its furniture is explored further in the next chapter.

1. Kim Han-kyo, ed., *Studies on Korea: A Scholar's Guide* (Honolulu: University Press of Hawaii, 1980), p. 176.

2. Kim Won-yong, "A Short History of Korean Crafts," in *Survey of Korean Arts: Fine Arts—I* (Seoul: National Academy of Arts, 1971), pp. 159–160.

3. Yanagi, Sōetsu, "The Mystery of Beauty: A Tribute to the Korean Craftsman," *Far Eastern Ceramic Bulletin* (September/December 1957), pp. 8–9. Yanagi has also commented on Korean crafts, among others, in Bernard Leach's edited collection of essays, *The Unknown Craftsman: A Japanese Insight into Beauty* (Tokyo: Kodansha International, 1972).

4. Ewha Womans University Museum, *Catalogue 9: Special Exhibition of Wooden Furniture of the Yi Dynasty* (Seoul: Ewha Womans University Museum, May 1980), p. 80.

5. See, among others, William Henthorn, *A History of Korea* (New York: Macmillan Publishing Co., Inc., 1971); John Somerville, "Stability in Eighteenth Century Ulsan," *Korean Studies Forum*, Volume I, Number 1, 1977; and Bae-ho Hahn, "The Authority Structure of Korean Politics," in E. R. Wright, ed., *Korean Politics in Transition* (Seattle: University of Washington Press, 1975), pp. 285–319. Henthorn's history survey illuminates the principal tenets of Yi political, economic, and social life. Somerville has shown that there was substantial breakdown in the exclusivity of the *yangban* as a class by the latter part of the dynasty. Hahn has given a clear and concise analysis of the class and group structure as it related to politics and government. Other insights have been gleaned from Michael Rogers, Professor of Oriental Languages and History at the University of California, Berkeley, in private conversations.

6. Barbara Young in *Spirit of the Tiger: Folk Art of Korea*, catalogue of exhibit of Korean folk art and furniture at Thomas Burke Memorial Museum, Seattle, December 5, 1979–March 28, 1980.

NOTE

The plate captions indicate size and material as well as approximate age and provenance. Rarely is the history of a piece known with certainty, so in some cases age and provenance are educated guesses. In most instances, provenance is determined on the basis of design and materials used.

Korean provinces were not administratively divided into north and south until relatively modern times, so it is not always possible to pinpoint origins to the north or south of Kyŏngsang, Ch'ŭngch'ŏng, or Chŏlla provinces. At least in style, most pieces pictured are assumed to be nineteenth century, though some are eighteenth and others early twentieth century. These questions are discussed in greater detail in the Introduction.

The McCune-Reischauer romanization system is directed principally toward accurate pronunciation. The one diacritical mark (ˇ) is used over the *o* and *u*. In other words, there are two *o*'s and two *u*'s. The *o* without a mark is pronounced as in the English *boat* or *soak*. The *ŏ* is shorter, with no exact English equivalent; it is something like *uh* or *fun*. The *o* and *ŏ* are sometimes confused by Koreans and frequently by foreigners. The *u* has a pronunciation close to the vowels in *moon* and *soon*; the *ŭ* has no English equivalent, but is something like *ew* or the German *ö*. The two *u*'s are often confused by Westerners. Concerning consonants, *k*, *t*, *p*, and *ch* are aspirated when followed by an apostrophe (*k'*, *t'*, *p'*, and *ch'*).

In general, the McCune-Reischauer system has been used for romanization of Korean words, except in the case of proper names and words that have other commonly recognized spellings, such as the widely used *bandaji* instead of the technically correct *pandaji*. Contemporary Korean personal names as much as possible follow the style adopted by the person himself or herself. Ewha Woman's University officially employs the spelling "Womans" in its English name; this spelling appears in this book at the university's behest.

1. *Bandaji*
Persimmon wood, iron fittings, oil finish
Middle nineteenth century, South Chŏlla Province
H. 90, W. 107, D. 46 cm.

The opening extends all the way across the front. This piece comes from the same area as the one in Plate 2, and the decorative fittings are almost identical. The boards comprising the front panels must have come from an exceptionally large persimmon tree, making this an extremely rare piece of furniture. The dramatic decorative effect of the dark grain figures in persimmon wood, which are often used to give the impression of a landscape painting, is clearly seen here.

2. *Bandaji*

Pearwood, iron fittings
Nineteenth century, South Chŏlla Province
H. 80, W. 104, D. 44 cm.

This is a very rare piece because it is quite large and constructed of thick boards of pearwood. Usually pearwood is reserved for the framing of fine furniture, with panels of zelkova or persimmon used for their decorative grains. The stark effect of sparse black ironwork against the flat-toned, yellow pearwood is unusual in Korean furniture and has much appeal.

3. Yŏng-gwang *bandaji*

Persimmon wood front panels, iron fittings
Middle nineteenth century, South Chŏlla Province, Yŏng-gwang area
H. 100, W. 108, D. 48 cm.

The mirror-image persimmon panels beautifully display the dramatic play of this wood's dark grain figure. Compare this quiet piece with the persimmon chest in Plate 39.

4. Pyŏngyang *bandaji*
Limewood, yellow brass fittings, oil finish
Middle nineteenth century, Pyŏngyang city area
H. 85, W. 87, D. 44.5 cm.

The extensive metalwork, typical of pieces from the north
of the peninsula, is unusual in being of yellow rather than
white brass and in having no incised designs except on the
handles (compare Plate 32).

5. Two-level chest (*ich'ŭng jang*)

Maple panels, zelkova frame, yellow brass fittings; red lacquer on molding, black lacquer on door frames and bottom panels, oil finish on panels and sides

Early to middle nineteenth century, Ch'ungch'ŏng or

Kyŏnggi Province

H. 147, W. 112, D. 58 cm.

The red and black lacquer trim on this type of simple yet elegant and opulent chest means that it was for use by members of the extended royal family.

6. Three-level chest (*samch'ŭng jang*)
Red lacquer on wood, white brass fittings, mother-of-pearl inlay
Early twentieth century, Kyŏnggi Province
H. 151.6, W. 91.8, D. 46.2 cm.
Collection: Ewha Womans University Museum

While this chest has the traditional shape and proportions of Yi furniture, the elaborate mother-of-pearl inlay would hardly have been found before this century on such a large piece. It was made for the women's quarters of a latter-day *yangban* household. Despite its dazzling gaudiness, there is something gentle and endearing about this piece. And some of the detail is wonderful.

7. Four-level chest (*sach'ŭng jang*)

Painted ox horn (*hwagak*) front panels on wood, paulownia sides and top, yellow brass fittings, oil finish
Nineteenth century, Kyŏnggi Province
H. 95.5, W. 52.5, D. 31 cm.
Collection: Ewha Womans University Museum

The painted ox horn panels are replete with happiness and longevity motifs. Some of the panels have deteriorated badly, probably because of moisture. It is a good example of why few old ox horn pieces now extant are in good condition. The piece is quite small for a four-level chest and was used in the women's quarters probably as a combination *mŏrijang* and *pŏsŏnjang* (for padded white socks).

8. Two-unit stacked chest (*ich'ŭng nong*)

Red lacquer on wood, yellow brass fittings
Nineteenth century, Kyŏnggi Province
H. 110, W. 70.5, D. 37.5 cm.

A lacquered chest of this kind is rare enough to be considered an important piece. To judge by the color, the red lacquer is a mixture of cinnabar and iron oxide pigments. The mottling is an unusual effect that deserves further study.

9. Two-unit stacked chest (*ich'ŭng nong*)

Paper on wood, iron fittings, oil finish
Nineteenth century, probably Ch'ungch'ŏng Province
H. 85 (without stand), W. 70.5, D. 36.5 cm.

Paper on wood, with or without decoration, finished with perilla oil is not unusual on wedding boxes and is sometimes seen on stacked chests and wardrobe chests. Such paper-covered chests do not seem to have been made in the Seoul area, but come from areas south of that city.

34

10. Two-unit stacked chest (*ich'ŭng nong*)

Colored and cut paper on wood, iron fittings, oil finish
Nineteenth century, probably Ch'ungch'ŏng Province
H. 75 (without stand), W. 52, D. 26 cm.

The grain of the wood beneath is clearly visible on the paper covering this chest. The decoration is subdued, consisting of a few decorative medallions, some red areas, and black lines simulating the type of molding found on framed chests (see Plate 6). Age has mellowed this piece, softening the colors and increasing its interest.

11. Headside chest (*mŏrijang*)

Zelkova burl panels, pine frame and molding, yellow brass fittings, oil finish
Early to middle nineteenth century, Chŏlla Province
H. 78.5, W. 112, D. 48 cm.

The mirror-image burl panels have been used to create an effect that is dynamic yet quietly elegant. The generous use of zelkova burl is an unusual feature of this piece from the southwestern part of the peninsula. It is considerably wider than the prototypic Kyŏnggi Province piece in Plate 14.

12. Headside chest (*mŏrijang*)

Painted and cut paper on wood, yellow brass fittings, oil finish
Nineteenth century, Chungch'ŏng Province
H. 60, W. 76, D. 32 cm.

This delightful folk piece is nothing more than a box with two doors—the "drawers" are painted decoration. Almost the entire front surface of this chest is decorated—with cut-paper appliqué, stenciled patterns, and freely drawn designs. The vigor of this decoration is compelling; when new it must have been brightly colored. Pieces of this kind are very rare. No studies of these paper-covered chests and their decoration are known to the authors, and it is an area that could be fruitfully explored. The decoration and motifs seem to hint at meaning, but may be just a combining of stylized design elements. The door designs, at least, are the Taoist *t'aeguk* motif.

13. Headside chest (*mŏrijang*)

Red and black lacquered wood, yellow brass fittings
Middle to late nineteenth century, Kanghwa Island (near Seoul)
H. 87.5, W. 90, D. 44 cm.

This chest style and colored lacquer finish were reserved for use by
members of the extended royal family.

14. Headside chest (*mŏrijang*)

Zelkova burl front panels, pearwood frame and molding, paulownia
    sides and top, yellow brass fittings

Late eighteenth to early nineteenth century, Suwŏn city, Kyŏnggi
    Province

H. 71, W. 71.5, D. 44 cm.

This is a beautifully constructed piece for the women's quarters and
can be considered a prototype of an upper-class headside chest, with
its low center of gravity and careful construction using three prized
woods.

15. Document and stationery boxes (*mungap*)

Persimmon wood panels, red oak (Chinese cedrela) frame, yellow
    brass fittings, oil finish

Late nineteenth to early twentieth century, Chŏlla or Kyŏngsang
    Province

H. 38.5, W. 95, D. 28 cm.

With this style of document and stationary box, the front panels lift
up and out, usually from one position only. In each box of the pair
pictured, the lift-up position is the second panel from the right, the
usual place in boxes of this kind. After this panel is removed, the
other panels are slid to this spot and lifted out.

16. Combination mirror and incidentals box (*kyŏngdae yŏnsang*) with matching tobacco box (*tambae gap*)

Persimmon wood, yellow brass fittings, oil finish

Middle to late nineteenth century, Seoul

Mirror-incidentals box: H. 27.5, W. 36, D. 25.5 cm.

Tobacco box: H. 9.5, W. 10.5, D. 13.5 cm.

This rare set for a *yangban* woman's use combines the functions of a mirror box with storage space for incidentals, including a space under the top-right panel for an inkstone. The matching tobacco box is very rare.

17. Ox horn box (*hwagak ham*)

Painted ox horn (*hwagak*) panels on wood, yellow brass fittings

Nineteenth century, Kyŏnggi Province

H. 14.5, W. 21.7, D. 21.7 cm.

Collection: Ewha Womans University Museum

This brightly colored and decorated box was for the women's quarters and was used for incidentals and small valuables. Most conspicuous in the panels are dragons, deer, flowers, and clouds. The *hwagak* process (see page 151) is still practiced in Korea, but boxes of this age are rare.

18. Women's incidentals boxes, primarily for combs
and hairpins (*pit-chŏp*)

Black lacquer on wood, mother-of-pearl inlay, yellow
brass fittings
Nineteenth century, South Kyŏngsang Province
Left: H. 28, W. 27.5, D. 25.5 cm.
Right: H. 26.5, W. 24, D. 23 cm.

The pairs of birds on the left-hand box symbolize
marital bliss, while the hexagonal pattern is known as
the tortoiseshell pattern and is a symbol of longevity,
as are the bat-shaped drawer pulls. The stylized character on the right-hand box is the character for longevity,
but the meaning of the highly stylized trees, if any,
is obscure.

19. Wedding boxes (*ham*)

Painted paper on wood, iron fittings, oil finish
Late nineteenth to early twentieth century, Ch'ungch'ŏng Province
H. 23.5, W. 66.5, D. 37 cm. each

This matching pair is unique, with its veritable forest of flowers and Taoist *t'aeguk* motifs on the fronts. The color tones are muted, so that the impression is not harsh or overwhelming. The front handles and iron lock plates are simple for wedding boxes, but appropriate for this ornate decoration.

20. Wedding boxes (*ham*)

Paper on wood, iron fittings, oil finish
Middle to late nineteenth century, Ch'ungch'ŏng or Chŏlla Province
H. 38, W. 58.5, D. 33 cm. each

The attached feet seen here are rare on wedding boxes, which are usually placed on top of a chest, not on the heated Korean floor. The monochrome simplicity of this paper is a sharp contrast with the intricate painting seen in Plate 19.

21, 22. Safe (*kap-kae suri*)
Zelkova burl, yellow brass fittings, oil finish
Middle to late nineteenth century, Kyŏnggi Province
H. 41, W. 51.5, D. 35 cm.

The yellow brass set against the swirl of wood grain results in an impressive composition. The space inside the piece is filled with drawers. The base appears to be a recent addition.

23. Coin chest (*ton-kwe*)
Pine wood, iron fittings, oil finish
Early nineteenth century; this chest is from Kyŏnggi Province, but is typical of a style found throughout the south
H. 54, W. 123, D. 58 cm.

This money chest is unusually massive and handsome and therefore must have belonged to a quite wealthy family. The combination of brass and iron in the top decorative nails is unusual.

24. Pair of medicine chests (*yakchang*)

Paulownia wood drawers, zelkova wood chest body,
   limewood drawer frames, yellow brass fittings, oil finish
Early to middle nineteenth century, Kyŏnggi Province
H. 50, W. 36, D. 30 cm. each

A matching pair of this kind is a rare find. The three kinds
of wood serve to add strength to such chests, with the
paulownia used for its insect-repelling quality and the
zelkova for its hardness. The drawer frames are unusually
delicate and finely constructed.

25. Book storage chest (*ch'aek mŏrijang*)

Zelkova wood, iron fittings
Early nineteenth century, Kyŏnggi Province
H. 72.5, W. 93, D. 41.5 cm.

This style of book chest with upturned ends on the top has Chinese
origins. The balanced zelkova wood panels are subtle yet spectacular.
The doors slide to each side rather than open outward.

26. Buddhist study or sutra desk (*kyŏngsang*)

Red lacquer on wood
Nineteenth century, Seoul
H. 28.5, W. 61, D. 28 cm.
Collection: Ewha Womans University Museum

That this elaborate Buddhist study desk finished with red lacquer is most unusual—such desks normally have a subdued, oil finish. The front carving is seen as a stylization of a bat. The upturned ends are not only decorative but help to prevent scrolls from rolling off the table. The legs are a variation of what are known as "tiger" legs.

27. Four-level chest (*sach'ŭng jang*)

Top: zelkova burl doors surrounded by persimmon panels;
   middle: zelkova doors and panels; bottom: persimmon
   doors and panels; chest frame and molding: zelkova;
   yellow brass fittings; oil finish
Late eighteenth to early nineteenth century, Seoul
H. 148.5, W. 101.5, D. 44.5 cm.

One of the many unusual aspects of this unique chest is that
the bottom doors hide medicine drawers (see Plate 24). This
finely constructed piece is reputed to have belonged to a
member of the Yi royal family. The decorative, almost
playful, use of two contrasting wood grains creates a rhythm
that captures the attention and keeps the eye in movement,
offering a subtle combination designed to be savored. The
top empty shelf compartment is relatively rare. The outer
hinges on the upper doors are a recent addition (1967).

28. *Bandaji*
Limewood, iron fittings
Early to middle nineteenth century, Kyŏnggi Province
H. 84.5, W. 95.5, D. 46.5 cm.
Collection: Mr. and Mrs. Peter Jhun

The metalwork is both finely wrought and unusually thick, like a low relief. The metal piece in the lower right-hand corner is a replacement.

29. *Bandaji*
Limewood, iron fittings, refinished
Middle nineteenth century,
  Kyŏnggi Province
H. 60, W. 83, D. 35.5 cm.

This piece is one of a matching pair, a rarity in itself. Most *bandaji* of this shape are set upon two simple boards to lift the chest off the heated floor, but this chest has "roll" feet, which extend from front to back on each side.

30. *Bandaji*
Probably limewood, iron fittings,
  oil finish
Nineteenth century, Kyŏnggi
  Province
H. 67, W. 88, D. 40 cm.

This chest, similar to those in Plates 28 and 29, was found on Cheju Island in 1978. It is clearly of Kyŏnggi Province type, presenting a mystery regarding how and when it arrived on Cheju. It has been cleaned and freshly oiled, though not refinished.

31. *Ssung-ssung-i bandaji*

Pine wood, iron fittings, thin red pigment visible under ironwork, where finish has not
   been scrubbed

Middle nineteenth century, Pakch'ŏn area

H. 77, W. 84, D. 41 cm.

The *ssung-ssung-i* style, from the northern part of the peninsula, is characterized by fine,
lacelike ironwork on the front of the chest. The central metal piece is a South Gate motif.

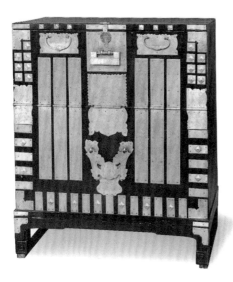

32. Pyŏngyang *bandaji*
Limewood, white brass fittings, oil finish
Middle nineteenth century, Pyŏngyang City area
H. 105.5, W. 90, D. 46 cm.

The incised designs on the brass on this northern piece include the usual melange of auspicious motifs—here, phoenix, pine trees, and flowers and rocks. Pyŏngyang *bandaji* are found in provinces in the south. The Korean War resulted in a large migration of people from north to south, many families taking along their chests and belongings.

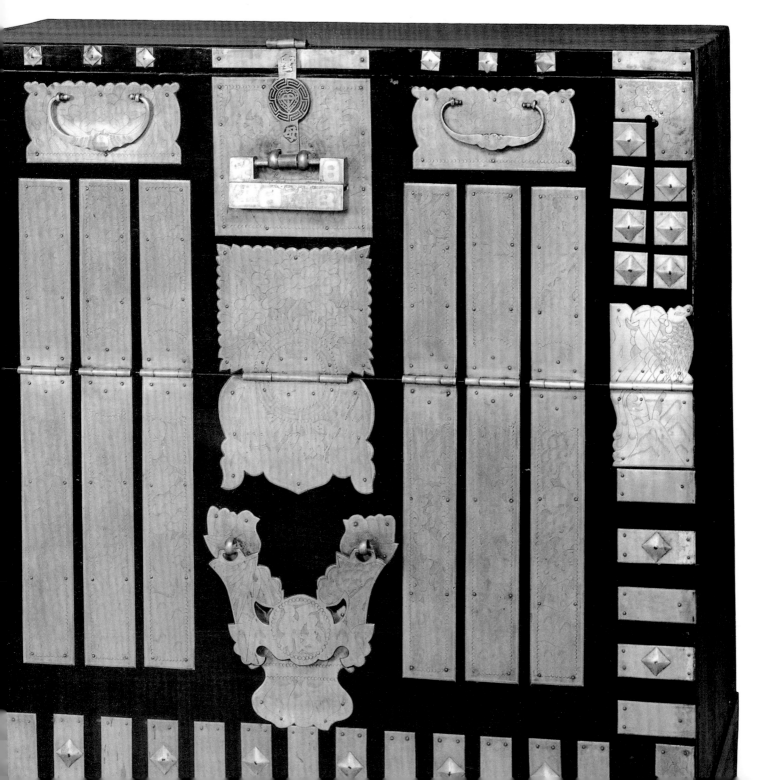

33. Yŏng-gwang *bandaji*

Maple wood panels, pine wood frame, iron fittings, oil finish

Middle nineteenth century, Yŏnggwang area, South Chŏlla Province

H. 96.5, W. 108.5, D. 48 cm.

This *bandaji* has a relatively small front opening, and the legs are carved with Chinese fret motifs. Yŏng-gwang *bandaji* normally have small drawers across the top, a feature not usually found on other *bandaji* types. The maple panels provide a more colorful effect than usually found with this chest style.

34. Chŏnju chest (*Chŏnju bandaji*)

Zelkova burl front, pine sides and top, iron fittings

Probably eighteenth century, Chŏnju city area, North Chŏlla Province

H. 102, W. 90, D. 39 cm.

The Chŏnju chest is characterized by a double-door opening above and a *bandaji*-type opening below. This quite old piece also has small drawers at the top. Its condition is excellent, perhaps because of the sturdy hinges and numerous staples (compare Plate 138).

35. Cheju Island *bandaji*
Zelkova wood, iron fittings, oil finish
Early to middle nineteenth century, Cheju Island
H. 58, W. 80, D. 40.5 cm.
Collection: Mr. and Mrs. Ben Kremenak

The metalwork on this piece typifies Cheju Island design; similar pieces are sometimes found in nearby coastal areas of the peninsula. The boards used remain unsmoothed, and the top, in fact, boasts large blemishes in the wood. This is a vigorous folk piece with much appeal.

36. *Sŏm* ("island") *bandaji*
Limewood, yellow brass fittings, oil finish
Late nineteenth to early twentieth century, coastal area of South Chŏlla Province
H. 47.5, W. 72.5, D. 35.5 cm.

This chest style was popular in the south coastal area in relatively humble households, which depended on the sea for a livelihood. Some see the hinges as stylized fish tails, though they have commonly been called variations of the swallowtail shape.

37. Pair of small or "baby" (*al*) *bandaji*
Zelkova wood, iron fittings, refinished
Middle to late nineteenth century, Kyŏnggi Province
H. 51, W. 51, D. 26 cm.

These small chests have iron fittings in the swallowtail shape. This pair is of traditional styling, but there is the possibility that they have been reconstructed from pieces of old chests. They have at least been scrubbed and freshly finished. Some Korean workshops can reproduce original styles and construction so well that even the experienced observer has difficulty in distinguishing the original from the reproduction.

38. Wardrobe chest (ŭigŏri-jang)

Paulownia wood panels, pearwood frame, iron
    fittings, oil finish
Middle to late nineteenth century, Ch'ung-
    ch'ŏng or Kyŏnggi Province
H. 156, W. 70.5, D. 35.5 cm.

This kind of wardrobe chest was a luxury of
upper-class families. Paulownia wood is
considered to be moisture proof and bug resistant, much as cedar is in the West. The
stolid simplicity of this piece is reminiscent of
Chinese designs, of which this is surely a very
Korean adaptation.

39. Two-unit, stacked wardrobe chest (ŭigŏri-
    jang)

Persimmon wood front panels, pearwood
    frame, paulownia sides, white brass fittings,
    oil finish
Early twentieth century, Kyŏnggi Province
    or city of Seoul
H. 154 (without stand), W. 94, D. 42 cm.

The spectacular contrasts of the mirror-image
persimmon panels, together with the white
brass hardware, make this chest design nothing
less than wild. It challenges the eye boldly and
joyfully. How it must have looked in the sedate
interior of an upper-class house is somehow
hard to envision.

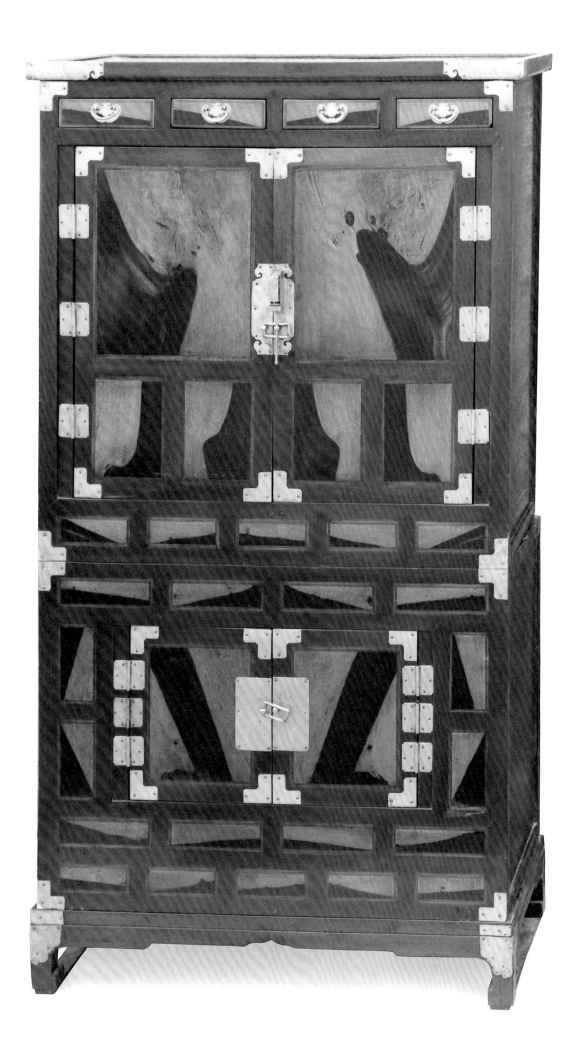

40. Two-unit stacked chest (*ich'ŭng nong*)
Paulownia wood, yellow brass fittings, oil finish
Early nineteenth century, Kyŏnggi Province
H. 87.5, W. 72, D. 37 cm.

This venerable chest is in completely original condition. It can be considered to be a prototype of the two-unit stacked chest. Such chests are made of thin boards, so fittings are commonly used to reinforce the relatively frail structure.

41. Two-unit stacked chest (*ich'ŭng nong*)
Paulownia wood, iron fittings, oil finish
Late nineteenth century, Kyŏngsang or Kyŏnggi Province
H. 96, W. 77, D. 34 cm.

The butterfly fittings in iron are unusual on a simple paulownia chest of this kind.

42. Two-unit stacked chest (*ich'ŭng nong*)
Persimmon door panels, paulownia wood,
  yellow brass fittings, oil finish
Late nineteenth to early twentieth century,
  South Kyŏngsang Province
H. 97.5, W. 79, D. 37 cm.

Not infrequently, stacked chests of quiet
paulownia wood are highlighted by dramatic
doors of persimmon.

43. Two-unit stacked chest (*ich'ŭng
    nong*)
Bamboo slats on wood, yellow brass
fittings, oil finish
Nineteenth century, Kyŏnggi Province
H. 93.5, W. 75.9, D. 39.3 cm.
Collection: Ewha Womans University
  Museum

Chests with bamboo slats or strips
fitted and glued into patterns over a
wooden base represent a genre of Korean
furniture. Most pieces on the market
today are reproductions, albeit usually
excellently crafted. The chest illustrated
is exceptionally rare for this fragile
bamboo work, being over a century
old. Bamboo is not as durable as wood,
and, also, the strips tend to warp and
peel off with temperature change. The
other bamboo piece represented here
is seen in Plate 123.

44. Two-unit stacked chest (*ich'ŭng nong*)

Zelkova burl front panels, zelkova frame, paulownia sides and top, yellow brass fittings

Early twentieth century, Kyŏnggi or North Kyŏngsang Province

H. 99 (without stand), W. 77, D. 37 cm.

The metalwork on this piece for an upper-class women's room (*anbang*) displays forms considered to be symbols of felicity and joy—the drawer pulls are bats, and the hinges and locks are butterflies.

45. Two-unit stacked chest (*ich'ŭng nong*)

Black lacquer on pine wood base, yellow brass fittings, mother-of-pearl inlay

Middle nineteenth century, Kyŏnggi Province

H. 92.5, W. 79, D. 38.5 cm.

Collection: Koryŏ University Museum

Tigers, dragons, pine, plum, and bamboo, rock, fungus—this piece is rife with auspicious designs. The craftsmanship is excellent, yet the inlaid decoration never gets finicky or cloying. The direct boldness has its own charm and is very Korean. The combination of tiger and dragon signifies protection and repelling of evil; this has not been forgotten, even in today's Korea.

46. Headside chest (*mŏrijang*)
Persimmon wood panels, pearwood frame, yellow brass fittings, oil finish
Late nineteenth to early twentieth century, Seoul
H. 59, W. 77, D. 34 cm.
Collection: Mrs. Pongsoon Lee

Drawers and front panels are framed with a line of dark inlaid wood, and the double-happiness characters are also inlaid wood. This rather sumptious piece is from the women's quarters of an upper-class home.

47. Headside chest (*mŏrijang*)
Persimmon wood on top front, pine wood, iron fittings, oil finish
Late nineteenth century, South Chŏlla Province
H. 91, W. 98.5, D. 47.5 cm.

Access to the generous interior of this elegantly styled chest is through the double doors at the top, not the most convenient arrangement if one wants to get at something on the bottom of the inside.

48, 49. Headside chest (*mŏrijang*)

Carved and lacquered wood, pine wood stand, yellow
  brass fittings

Eighteenth century, Kyŏnggi Province

H. 60, W. 53.5, D. 33 cm.

Collection: National Museum of Korea

This intricately carved piece is a sharp contrast with the
majority of Korean furniture pieces, yet it is unequivocally
Korean. It is possible that this was made by different craftsmen, one each specializing in cabinetry, carving, and lacquering.

50. Hat box (*t'ang-gon tong*)
Paulownia wood, yellow brass fittings, oil finish
Middle to late nineteenth century, Ch'ungch'ŏng or Chŏlla Province
H. 37.5, Diam. 47 cm.

This box for storing a man's hat is designed to be hung from the loop on the top; the lid
is the bottom.

51. Octagonal hat box (*kwansang*)
Persimmon wood, yellow brass fittings, oil finish
Late nineteenth to early twentieth century, Seoul
H. 22, W. 36 cm.
Collection: Mrs. Seyong Kim

It is unusual to find this kind of man's hat box made of precious and decorative persimmon wood. The craftsmanship of this piece is excellent, and a generous use of brass adds to the sumptious effect.

52. Hat and formal clothing box (*kwan-bok ham*)
Paulownia wood, yellow brass fittings, oil finish
Middle nineteenth century, Kyŏnggi or Ch'ungch'ŏng Province
H. 37, W. 27.5, D. 16.5 cm.

This box is for storing a man's special dress clothing (in this case it contained formal wedding attire), including the man's traditional hat made of lacquered horsehair mesh.

53. Document box (*sŏryu ham*)
Brownish red lacquer on lime-
wood, yellow brass fittings
Middle to late nineteenth century,
South Kyŏngsang Province
H. 14, W. 57.5, D. 33.5 cm.

The curved top of this box is
unusual. It may have been used as
a gift box (*yemul ham*); in such a
case, the contents constituted the
gift, and the box normally would
have been returned to the giver.

54. Document box (*sŏryu ham*)
Pine wood, yellow brass fittings
Late nineteenth century, South
Kyŏngsang Province
H. 19.5, W. 42.5, D. 42.5 cm.

**55. Document and incidentals box
(*mokkap*)**
Korean ash wood, yellow brass
fittings, oil finish
Eighteenth century, Kyŏnggi
Province
H. 8.2, W. 9.3, D. 16.3 cm.
Collection: Ewha Womans
University Museum

Korean ash was not widely used
in Yi dynasty furniture, probably
because of limited availability.
This small box shows it off to best
advantage.

56. Document boxes (*sŏryu ham*)

Leather on wood, yellow brass fittings (on right), lacquer finish

Nineteenth century, Ch'ungch'ŏng or Kyŏnggi Province

Left: H. 13, W. 44, D. 24 cm.

Right: H. 17, W. 38, D. 19 cm.

Usually small document boxes were made of wood alone, but occasionally one encounters leather-covered pieces such as these. Paper-covered boxes are also found.

57. Document box (*sŏryu ham* or *munso ham*)

Ginkgo wood, iron fittings, oil finish

Early nineteenth century, probably Kyŏnggi Province

H. 11.5, W. 61, D. 18 cm.

The shape of the carved openings is referred to as "elephant eye." How this box was used is a matter of conjecture. The long shape suggests a scroll case (*yongjong ham*), but it may have been a gift box (*yemul ham*).

58. Document and stationery box (*mungap* or *sŏryu ham*)

Black lacquer on ginkgo wood, yellow brass fittings, mother-of-pearl inlay

Middle nineteenth century, Chungmu (formerly T'ongyŏng) city area, South Kyŏngsang Province

H. 10.9, W. 33.2, D. 15.6 cm.

Collection: National Museum of Korea

Lacquered boxes with mother-of-pearl inlay have a long history in Korea, but the number of extant pieces is quite small, making accurate dating difficult.

59. Document and stationery box (*mungap*)
Paulownia wood, yellow brass fittings
Nineteenth century, South Kyŏngsang Province
H. 32, W. 33.5, D. 27 cm.

The front panel lifts up and out to reveal four pigeonhole compartments. The usual style of document box is the kind seen in Plates 15 and 60; this simple little box with a single panel is a rarity.

60. Document and stationery box (*mungap*)
Zelkova burl panels; zelkova frame, top, and sides; yellow brass fittings
Late nineteenth to early twentieth century, Chŏlla or Kyŏngsang Province
H. 34.5, W. 73, D. 28 cm.

61. Stationery and incidentals tray (*mungap yŏnsang*)
Maple panels surrounded by wood inlay, zelkova frame, white brass fittings, oil finish, black lacquered tray interior
Middle nineteenth century, Chungmu city, South Kyŏngsang Province
H. 26, W. 70, D. 35.5 cm.

This style of stationery box has a tray on the top for holding an inkstone, smoking utensils, or other incidentals. The tray and the drawers (on the other side of the box) are also for paper, brushes, and other writing materials. The piece is carefully finished on all sides. Of particular interest is the delicate wood inlay pattern surrounding the maple panels.

62. Document and stationery box (*mungap*)
Zelkova wood, yellow brass fittings, oil finish
Middle to late nineteenth century, South Kyŏngsang Province
H. 30, W. 80, D. 31 cm.

This handy storage box has an open compartment as well as a panel on the top left covering a space for inkstone and brushes.

63. Mirror and cosmetics box (*mal kyŏngdae*)
Lacquer on ginkgo wood, white brass fittings
Late nineteenth century, Chinju city area, South Kyŏngsang Province
H. 28, W. 25, D. 32 cm.

This piece illustrates the typical shape of the Korean mirror box, which could hold cosmetics, combs, hairpins, or whatever.

64. Women's combs and incidentals boxes (*pit-chŏp*)
Paulownia wood, yellow brass fittings, oil finish
Nineteenth century, South Kyŏngsang Province
Left: H. 29.5, W. 25, D. 25 cm.
Right: H. 24, W. 25, D. 25 cm.

The left box has a bottom drawer, while the right one does not—the bat-shaped handle is purely decorative.

65. Sewing box (*panjit kŭrŭt* or *panjit-kori*)
Pine wood, oil finish
Late nineteenth to early twentieth century, South Kyŏngsang Province
H. 11, W. 38, D. 39 cm.

Such boxes were found in the women's inner room. The small compartment is for needles and thread.

66. Sewing box (*panjit kŭrŭt* or *panjit-kori*)
Painted ox horn (*hwagak*) on paulownia wood
Middle nineteenth century, Kyŏnggi Province
H. 6.1, W. 28.2, D. 27.1 cm.
Collection: National Museum of Korea

Furniture adorned with painted ox horn was owned by royalty or the cream of the upper class. That this fragile decoration was used on a utility box to hold sewing materials is probably a testament to the exalted position of the piece's owner. The quarters of upper-class women were generally colorful, and the bright flowers on this box, reminiscent of flowers seen in screen and scroll paintings, would fit such surroundings.

67. Jewelry boxes (p'ae-mul ham)
Red and black lacquer on wood, yellow brass fittings
Late nineteenth to early twentieth century, Chŏlla Province
Left and right (pair): H. 20, W. 29.5, D. 19.5 cm.
Center: H. 14, W. 24, D. 15 cm.

Such small boxes were often used for jewelry, but undoubtedly were used for other women's incidentals as well. The Ewha University Museum simply classifies such pieces as "boxes."

68. Mirror and cosmetics box (mal kyŏngdae)
Red lacquer on ginkgo wood, yellow brass fittings
Middle nineteenth century, Chinju city or Chungmu (formerly T'ongyŏng) city, South Kyŏngsang Province
H. 30, W. 24.5, D. 34.5 cm.
Collection: Koryŏ University Museum

This is a representative example of red-lacquered mirror and cosmetic boxes. Often the brass fittings are larger and much more ornate.

69. Mirror box (kyŏngdae)
Ginkgo door panels, zelkova wood, yellow brass fittings, oil finish
Middle nineteenth century, Seoul area, Kyŏnggi Province
H. 18.5, W. 21, D. 27 cm.

This elegant little box is from the inner room (anbang) of a lady of an upper-class household. The mirror fits underneath the lid and lifts up, as seen in Plate 63.

70. Wedding box (*ham*)
Clear lacquer on wood, yellow brass
 fittings
Nineteenth century, Kyŏnggi Province
H. 22, W. 67.5, D. 38.5 cm.

The motifs around the circumference of the
back plate for the lock are stylizations of
the magic fungus (*pulloch'o*) that is a symbol
of longevity.

71. Wedding box (*ham*)
Black lacquer on wood, yellow brass
 fittings
Late nineteenth century, Kyŏnggi
 Province
H. 22.5, W. 68.5, D. 39 cm.

The motifs surrounding the lock plate
and the lock catch itself are both stylizations of the *pulloch'o* fungus, also seen
in Plate 70. Inside each fungus motif is
a five-petaled floral form, which echoes
the incised plum blossom motif inside the
roundel of the lock plate.

72. Wedding box (*ham*)
Pine wood, white brass fittings, natural
 lacquer finish
Late nineteenth to early twentieth century,
 South Kyŏngsang Province
H. 44, W. 72, D. 35 cm.

73. Pair of wedding boxes (*ham*)
Paper on wood, yellow brass fittings and trim, natural lacquer finish
Late nineteenth to early twentieth century, South Kyŏngsang Province
H. 28 (without feet), W. 57, D. 27.5 cm.

An unusual feature of this matching pair is the brass trim. These have been constructed so that the top is the box lid, which is removed by a fingerhole in the middle.
This lid structure is unique in the experience of the authors.

74, 75. Wedding box (*ham*)
Black lacquer on wood, white brass
  fittings
Late nineteenth to early twentieth
  century, Chŏlla Province
H. 44, W. 82, D. 38 cm.

The Chinese characters in the two medallions are for happiness (left) and
longevity. Incised into the lock plate
are various auspicious motifs such as
pine, bamboo, deer, crane, rocks, and
magic fungus. The hinges on the back,
in the form of the South Gate motif,
display incised characters and plants.

76. Pair of wedding boxes (*ham*)
Paper on wood, iron fittings, natural lacquer finish
Nineteenth century, Ch'ungch'ŏng Province
H. 37.5, W. 62, D. 30 cm.

77. Coin chest (*ton-kwe*)
Zelkova wood, iron fittings, oil finish
Nineteenth century, Kyŏnggi Province
H. 40, W. 86, D. 41.75 cm.

78. Coin chest (*ton-kwe*)
Pine wood, iron fittings, oil finish
Nineteenth century, Chŏlla Province
H. 48.5, W. 76, D. 48 cm.

This coin chest, like the one in Plate 79, has no hinges. The lid is constructed so that it lifts out completely yet cannot be opened when the front clasp is locked.

79. Coin chest (*ton-kwe*)
Zelkova wood, iron fittings
Middle to late nineteenth century, Kyŏnggi Province
H. 41, W. 68.75, D. 36 cm.

80. Three-level kitchen cabinet (*samch'ŭng ch'an-jang*)
Zelkova front panels, pine frame and molding, iron fittings,
 oil finish
Early to middle nineteenth century, Kyŏnggi Province
H. 166, W. 113, D. 48 cm.

This is in fact a two-level cabinet on top of which another
unit is stacked to form the completed piece, though three
(sometimes two) levels within a single frame is the most
common type. In the early 1970s, reproduction kitchen
chests began to appear on the Seoul market; many sold
there now are new, though traditional in style, materials,
and construction. This piece was purchased by a private
collector in 1967. These kitchen cabinets rely on the use
of wood alone for their appeal and do not depend on
decorative metal fittings for effect.

81. Kitchen shelves (*ch'an sonban-jang* or *puŏk t'akja*)

Pine wood, oil finish
Middle nineteenth century, Kyŏnggi Province
H. 143, W. 92, D. 31 cm.
Collection: Mr. Han Ki-taek

The same style of shelf unit is seen in a genre painting by the eighteenth century artist Sin Yun-bok.

82. Kitchen cabinet with shelves (*puŏk t'akja* or *ch'an t'akja*)

Pine wood, oil finish
Middle nineteenth century, Kyŏnggi Province
H. 148, W. 72, D. 32 cm.
Collection: Mr. Han Ki-taek

83. Kitchen cabinet (*puŏk t'akja* or *ch'an t'akja*)

Pine wood, yellow brass fittings
Nineteenth century, Kyŏnggi Province
H. 92.5, W. 92.5, D. 38.5 cm.

This piece is similar to that in Plate 82, but without the upper portion. Unlike most kitchen cabinets, it has a brass rather than an iron lock plate. The single piece of metal beautifully sets off the cabinet's lines and proportions.

84. Two-level kitchen cabinet (*ich'ŭng ch'an-jang*)
Pine wood, iron fittings, refinished
Early nineteenth century or possibly earlier, probably Kyŏngsang or
   Ch'ungch'ŏng Province
H. 119, W. 116, D. 45 cm.

The exact use of this unusual old piece is still uncertain, but the chest
seems to state kitchen cabinet more than anything else. The odd,
large square drawers probably would not be for books, the height is
convenient for someone standing, and the construction of the top
corners echoes the construction of rice storage boxes (Plate 87).
Drawers show repairs in the wood, and the metalwork is considerably
younger than the wood. This is a utility chest, but one of great dignity
and beauty.

85. Kitchen chest with rice storage compartment (*tuiji-jang*)

Zelkova front panels and molding, pine sides, iron fittings, oil finish

Middle nineteenth century, South Kyŏngsang Province

H. 66.5, W. 91, D. 39 cm.

Collection: Mr. Nam Goong

This rather elaborate little kitchen chest is suggestive of a book chest in shape and style, though a book chest would not have two such compartments with top and front openings. The top section, which opens by a hinged lid, is for rice storage, while the bottom is for storage of kitchen implements. The "animal" legs are also unusual on a kitchen piece.

86. Red bean storage box (*p'at tuiju*)

Zelkova panels, pine frame, iron fittings, oil finish

Middle nineteenth century, Kyŏnggi Province

H. 69.5, W. 63, D. 53.5 cm.

Larger sizes of this style of box were used to store rice. Rice and bean storage chests were kept in or adjacent to the kitchen. On both types, the front part of the top lifts off.

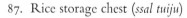

87. Rice storage chest (*ssal tuiju*)

Zelkova front panel, pine frame, iron fittings, oil finish

Nineteenth century; from Kyŏnggi or North Kyŏngsang Province, but of a style found throughout the peninsula

H. 80, W. 85.5, D. 58.5 cm.

This type of storage box is also seen in the eighteenth century genre painting by Sin Yun-bok. The handsome use of a large piece of zelkova for the front provides a decorative touch, where, pragmatically, none is necessary.

88. Tray-table (*soban* or, sometimes, *chuan-sang*)

Zelkova wood, natural lacquer finish

Middle to late nineteenth century; probably from Ch'ung-ch'ŏng Province, but this style is found throughout the south half of the peninsula

H. 24, Diam. 30.5 cm.

This *chuan* is small and was used for snacks and drinks rather than for a large meal. The legs are in the "tiger" style (*hochokban*). The term *chuan* refers to a table for serving wine or liquor, whereas *soban* is a general term for a tray-table for dining.

89. Tray-table (*soban*)

Ginkgo wood, oil finish

Late nineteenth to early twentieth century, Kyŏnggi or Kyŏngsang Province

H. 20.5, Diam. 45.5 cm.

Collection: Mr. and Mrs. R. Bailey Markham

This piece has an unusually large diameter. The shape is the prototype of tray-tables with the cabriole leg shape known as the "tiger" leg.

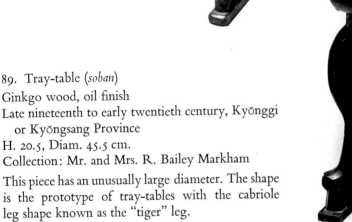

90. Tray-tables (*soban* or *hojok hwahyŏngban*)

Left: ginkgo wood, oil finish; Right: zelkova wood, oil finish

Late nineteenth or early twentieth century, Kyŏnggi or Kyŏngsang Province

Left: H. 20, Diam. 32.5 cm.

Right: H. 21.5, Diam. 32 cm.

91. Tray-tables (*soban*)

Left: pine wood, oil finish; Right: probably ginkgo wood, natural lacquer finish

Early twentieth century, Kyŏnggi or Kyŏngsang Province

Left: H. 27, Diam. 39.5–40.5 cm.

Right: H. 23.5, Diam. 37.5 cm.

Though made after the same basic pattern, the variation of detail and style in these *soban* is very great. These two examples are unusual variants. Both are artless and charming, but the photograph does not capture the chunky, vigorous construction of the piece on the right. The table on the left has what are known as "crane" legs.

92. Tray-table (*soban* or *hojok hwahyŏngban*)

Ginkgo wood, oil finish

Late nineteenth to early twentieth century, Kyŏnggi or Kyŏngsang Province

H. 25.5, Diam. 47–48 cm.

Like the piece in Plate 89, this has an unusually large diameter. The combination of foliate top and "tiger" legs is known as *hojok hwahyŏngban*.

93. Tray-table (*soban*)

Zelkova wood, oil finish

Nineteenth century, Kyŏnggi Province

H. 12.8, Diam. 29 cm.

Collection: Ewha Womans University Museum

This is a particularly low table, used to hold medicine and a water vessel. It is twelve sided and has "tiger" legs.

94. Tray-table (*soban* or *Naju-ban*)
Zelkova wood, natural lacquer finish
Late nineteenth century, Ch'ungch'ŏng or Kyŏnggi
  Province
H. 29, Diam. 44 cm.
Collection: National Museum of Korea

This is a piece of the finest workmanship from an upper-class home. The bars beneath the top identify this as being from the Naju area (see Plates 108–10).

95. Tray-table (*taegwŏl-ban*)
Red lacquer on ginkgo wood
Middle nineteenth century, Kyŏnggi Province or Seoul
H. 36.5, Diam. 70 cm.
Collection: Koryŏ University Museum

The style and color indicate that this rare lacquered table belonged to a high-ranking government official. The quality of carving on this piece is exceptional, and the foliate top is unusually thin.

96. Tray-table (*panwŏl-ban*)
Ginkgo wood, natural lacquer finish
Middle nineteenth century, Kyŏnggi Province
H. 27.5, W. 46, D. 36 cm.
Collection: National Museum of Korea

The practicality of this directional shape for serving food is clear enough, yet this three-legged piece is a very rare type.

97. Tray-table (*k'aedari soban*)
Zelkova wood, natural lacquer finish
Middle nineteenth century, Kyŏnggi Province
H. 42.5, Diam. 42.2 cm.
Collection: Mr. Han Ki-taek

The feet of this unusual and elegant piece turn in and are called "dog" legs (*k'aedari*). "Tiger" legs are cabriole and the feet turn out.

99. Round tray-tables (*chaeban*)
Zelkova or pine wood, natural lacquer finish
Late nineteenth or early twentieth century, Kangnung city, Kangwŏn Province
H. 10–12, Diam. 37–43 cm.

That such trays sometimes were turned from incompletely dried wood is seen in the warped piece in the middle. Regardless of warpage, such pieces were used. These all came from a single source, probably a temple.

98. Round tray-table (*chaeban*)
Ginkgo wood, oil finish
Middle to late nineteenth century, Kangnung city, Kangwŏn Province
H. 24, Diam. 41–43 cm.

This is a marvelous example of Korean turned wood. The vibrant energy and directness of Korean folkcraft is evident here at a glance.

100. Rectangular tray-table (*Haeju-ban*)
Pine wood, oil finish
Early twentieth century, identified with the area around
  Haeju city, South Hwanghae Province
H. 29, W. 44.5, D. 32.5 cm.

Plates 100–104 show a selection of the most basic, utilitarian types of *Haeju-ban*, each with a slightly different side opening.

101. Rectangular tray-table (*Haeju-ban*)
Pine wood, oil finish
Early twentieth century; identified with the area around
  Haeju city, South Hwanghae Province
H. 27, W. 44, D. 32.5 cm.

103. Rectangular tray-table (*Haeju-ban*)
Pine wood, oil finish
Early twentieth century, identified with the area around
  Haeju city, South Hwanghae Province
H. 27, W. 44, D. 33 cm.

102. Rectangular tray-table (*Haeju-ban*)
Ginkgo wood, oil finish
Early twentieth century; identified with the area around
  Haeju city, South Hwanghae Province
H. 35, W. 52, D. 33 cm.

104. Rectangular tray-table (*Haeju-ban*)
Ginkgo wood, natural lacquer finish
Early twentieth century; identified with the area around
  Haeju city, South Hwanghae Province
H. 27, W. 44, D. 33.5 cm.

105. Rectangular tray-table (*Haeju-ban*)
Ginkgo wood, oil finish
Late nineteenth century; identified with the area
   around Haeju city, South Hwanghae Province
H. 28, W. 45, D. 36 cm.
Collection: Mr. and Mrs. Yoong Bae

This is an excellent example of an upper-class *Haeju-ban*, with intricately carved floral panels.

106. Rectangular tray-table (*Haeju-ban*)
Ginkgo wood top, pine wood sides, oil finish
Early twentieth century; identified with the area
   around Haeju city, South Hwanghae Province
H. 25.5, W. 48, D. 36 cm.

The carvings in the side panels are the ubiquitous characters for felicity and long life.

107. Rectangular tray-table with "dog" legs (*kak kukjŏkban* or *k'aedari soban*)
Ginkgo wood, natural lacquer finish
Middle nineteenth century, Ch'ungch'ŏng Province
H. 30, W. 42.5, D. 36 cm.

The deep tray top raises questions regarding the possible uses of this tray-table. Perhaps it was an ancestral altar table (*chaesa soban*).

108. Rectangular tray-table with bamboo-shaped legs (*chukjŏl-ban*; also called *Naju-ban*)

Zelkova wood top, ginkgo wood legs, natural lacquer finish
Early twentieth century, South Chŏlla Province
H. 17.5, W. 45, D. 34 cm.

Bars or stretchers with a raised middle define the style of tray-table associated with the Naju city area (see Plates 94, 109, 110).

109. Rectangular tray-table with bamboo-shaped legs (*chukjŏl-ban* or *Naju-ban*) Zelkova wood, oil finish
Nineteenth century, South Chŏlla Province
H. 33, W. 78.3, D. 46.1 cm.
Collection: Ewha Womans University Museum
The carving and joinery of the openwork ends and sides represents the finest Korean woodworking.

110. Rectangular tray-table with bamboo-shaped legs (*chukjŏl-ban*; also called *chuan-sang*, a tray for snacks and drinks, and *Naju-ban*, after its style)

Ginkgo wood, natural lacquer finish
Late nineteenth to early twentieth century, Ch'ungch'ŏng Province
H. 41, W. 51, D. 38 cm.

This table, with its delicate lines and subtle proportions, is unusually tall.

111. Pedestaled tray-table (*soban* or *konggosang*)
Ginkgo wood, oil finish
Nineteenth century, Seoul
H. 27.5, Diam. 43.5 cm.
Collection: Ewha Womans University Museum

112. Pedestaled tray-table (*soban*)
Ginkgo wood, natural lacquer finish
Late nineteenth century, Kyŏnggi Province
H. 27, Diam. 41 cm.
Collection: Mr. Han Ki-taek

Each of the eight panels of the base contains a different carved design. This is a masterpiece of Korean craftsmanship.

113. Pedestaled tray-table (*chuch'il chisŭngban*)
Woven paper twine, lacquer finish
Late nineteenth to early twentieth century, Seoul area
H. 12.8, Diam. 36.4 cm.
Collection: Ewha Womans University Museum

Basketry objects made of paper twine, unfinished, oiled, or lacquered, form a minor but fascinating genre of Korean folkcrafts. Such objects are extremely durable and sturdy, especially if they have been lacquered. Here the craftsman has not only created a complex shape, but has embellished it with openwork on the base. Further, this piece is ten sided, a shape occasionally encountered in Korean objects, but not known to the authors from other folk traditions. Why ten sides?

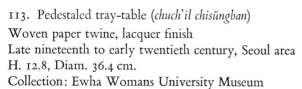

114. Pedestaled tray-table (*soban* or *iljuban*; the latter means "single bowl table")
Ginkgo wood, oil finish
Nineteenth century, Seoul area
H. 26.3, Diam. 37 cm.
Collection: Ewha Womans University Museum

This table was probably used for a water jar or for medicine or for both. This kind of elaborate carving is not usually found on serving tables of this type.

115. Pedestaled tray-table (*hoichŏn soban*)

Ginkgo wood, natural lacquer finish

Late nineteenth century, Kyŏnggi Province.

H. 45, Diam. 69 cm.

Collection: Koryŏ University Museum

The twelve-sided top of this table revolves, making this piece not only a fine piece of craftsmanship but a novelty as well. It is hypothesized that the late Yi dynasty saw more and more carving put into furniture. If this is correct, this table dates from that time.

116. Pedestaled tray-table (*soban* or *turiban*)

Ginkgo wood, oil finish

Nineteenth century, Seoul

H. 22, Diam. 56.8 cm.

Collection: Ewha Womans University Museum

This low twelve-sided table is of classic lines and proportions, without need of decoration.

117. Medicine chest (*yak-chang*)
Zelkova wood, yellow brass fittings, refinished
Middle to late nineteenth century, North Kyŏngsang Province
H. 87.5, W. 83, D. 33 cm.

This chest is rare in that it is divided into two tiers and fitted with the type of sliding doors seen on *mungap*-style document chests (Plate 60). Normally, a medicine chest is not so elegantly constructed; this piece is undoubtedly from a wealthy household. As is common with such chests, each drawer is inscribed with the name or names of the medicines within.

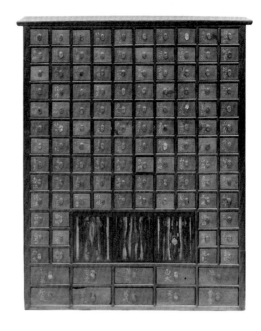

118. Medicine chest (*yak-chang*)

Limewood drawer fronts, three persimmon panels, pine wood frame,
  yellow brass handles

Middle to late nineteenth century, Kyŏnggi Province

H. 125, W. 45, D. 23 cm.

This exceptionally large family medicine chest has three *mungap*-style lift-up panels near the bottom. Surprisingly, more drawers for medicine are behind them.

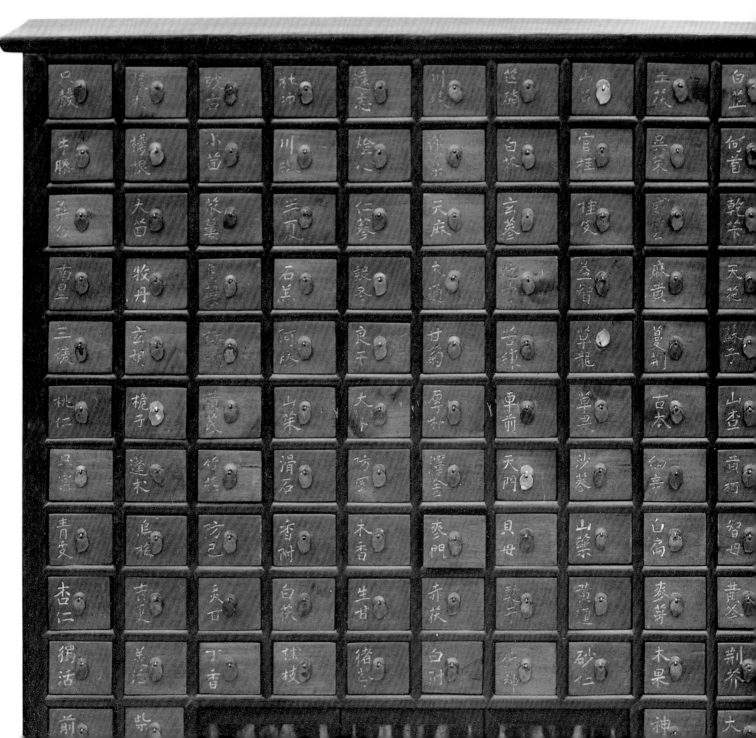

119. Summer bed (*p'yŏngsang*)
Pine wood, oil finish
Middle nineteenth century, Kyŏnggi or
   Ch'ungch'ŏng Province
H. 16, W. 252, D. 102 cm.

This summer bed is about as modest and basic as
such pieces come. The slats are pine, rather than the
more resilient bamboo seen in the piece below.

120. Summer bed (*p'yŏngsang*)
Zelkova wood frame, bamboo slats, yellow brass
   fittings, oil finish
Middle to late nineteenth century, Kyŏnggi
   Province
H. 31.5, W. 198, D. 99 cm.

Bamboo provides a resilience and spring that most
woods do not have when used in this manner. The
spaces between the slats allow the air to circulate in
the muggy Korean summer heat. Such beds were
used in the *sarang-bang* or on the porch of an upper-
class house.

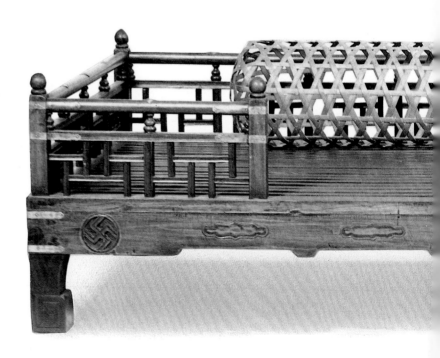

121. Summer bed (*p'yŏngsang*)
Zelkova wood, yellow brass fittings, oil finish,
   bamboo pillow and "bolster"
Late nineteenth century, southern half of peninsula
H. 45.5, W. 224, D. 88 cm.
Collection: Koryŏ University Museum

The slats of this bed run lengthwise rather than
across as in the other two examples included here.
The openwork rail, carving, and fancy metalwork
all proclaim this a luxury piece. The large bamboo
basketry object is called a "bamboo wife" (*chuk-
puin*).

94

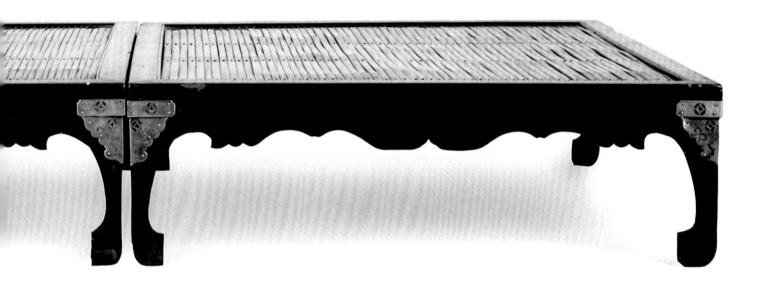

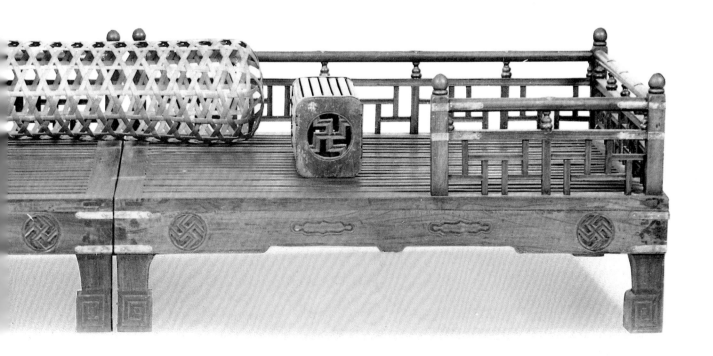

122. Four-level book storage and display stand (*sabang t'akja*)

Paulownia wood shelves, pine wood frame, oil finish

Middle nineteenth century, Kyŏnggi or Ch'ungch'ŏng Province

H. 149.5, W. 38.7, D. 38.7 cm.

Collection: National Museum of Korea

The lines of this stand are simple, but the proportions impeccable. Such pieces were used to display prized ceramics and art objects as well as to stack books.

123. Four-level book storage and display stand (*sabang-t'akja*)

Bamboo slats on wood, iron and yellow brass fittings, oil finish

Middle to late nineteenth century, Chŏlla Province

H. 148.5, W. 58, D. 30.5 cm.

Collection: Mr. Han Ki-taek

Few Yi dynasty bamboo pieces can be found in such good condition. Compare Plate 43.

124. Five-level book storage and display stand (*sabang t'akja*)

Paulownia wood panels, zelkova frame, yellow brass fittings, oil finish

Late nineteenth century, Kyŏnggi or Ch'ungch'ŏng Province

H. 178, W. 65.3, D. 31.8 cm.

Collection: National Museum of Korea

The construction of this five-level chest is exceptionally rare—in fact, it is unique in the authors' experience.

125. Four-level book storage and display stand (*sabang t'akja*)

Persimmon wood panels, paulownia shelves, pearwood frame, yellow brass fittings, oil finish

Late nineteenth to early twentieth century, Kyŏnggi Province

H. 160, W. 47.5, D. 32 cm.

The compartment on the bottom was usually used for book or manuscript storage; the shelves served a similar function or were for displaying treasured ceramics and curios. The grain design on the persimmon panels was carefully chosen and crafted to evoke the impression of a landscape.

126. Three-level book storage and display stand (*sabang t'akja*)

Persimmon wood panels, paulownia shelves, pearwood frame, yellow brass fittings, oil finish

Middle to late nineteenth century, Kyŏnggi or Ch'ungch'ŏng Province

H. 128, W. 47, D. 44 cm.

Collection: Koryŏ University Museum

127. Four-level book and manuscript storage chest (*sabang t'akja*)

Persimmon wood front panels, paulownia sides and shelves, pearwood frame and molding, yellow brass fittings, oil finish

Late nineteenth to early twentieth century, Kyŏnggi or North Kyŏngsang Province

H. 148, W. 44, D. 33 cm.

This chest was meticulously made for an upper-class household, utilizing three prized woods and persimmon panels in interesting arrangements of symmetry and assymetry.

128. Four-level book storage and display stand (*sabang t'akja*)
Paulownia wood panels, pine wood frame, sides, and back, oil finish
Nineteenth century, Kyŏnggi Province
H. 117.5, W. 54.8, D. 18 cm.
Collection: Ewha Womans University Museum

This unusual book storage cabinet was made for the men's quarters of an upper-class home. There is no metalwork, and the poem inscribed on the sliding panels makes one believe that the piece might have been owned by a gentleman-scholar, which very likely was the intent of its owner.

129. Bookcase and storage chest (*ch'aekchang*)
Paulownia wood, yellow brass fittings, oil finish
Middle to late nineteenth century, Chinju city area, South Kyŏngsang Province
H. 93, W. 69, D. 32 cm.
Collection: National Museum of Korea

This small bookcase for the men's quarters is entirely of paulownia wood and has "dog" legs (inturned feet and no hip). Taoist trigrams decorate the central metal lock plate.

130. Three-level book storage chest (*samch'ŭng ch'aekchang*)
Paulownia panels and sides, pearwood frame, yellow brass fittings, oil finish
Early twentieth century, Kyŏnggi Province
H. 136, W. 43.7, D. 36.5 cm.
Collection: Koryŏ University Museum

Traditional Korean books, as in China and Japan, were not hard bound. They had to be laid on their sides or be boxed in sets. Bookcases and storage chests were designed so that books could be stacked.

131. Book storage *bandaji* (*ch'aek bandaji*)
Pine wood, iron fittings, oil finish
Eighteenth century, Taegu city area, North Kyŏngsang Province
H. 50, W. 110, D. 22 cm.

The upturned ends on the top of this old *bandaji* characterize it as a chest for book and manuscript storage rather than for clothes.

132. Book storage chest (*ch'aek bandaji*)
Pine wood, iron fittings, oil finish
Nineteenth century, Chŏlla or Kyŏngsang Province
H. 44, W. 80.5, D. 30.5 cm.

133. Book storage chest (*ch'aek-sang*)
Pine wood, iron fittings, oil finish
Nineteenth century, Chŏlla or Kyŏnggi Province
H. 58, W. 93, D. 33 cm.
This chest has an unusual latch, which slides up into a groove in the top.

134. Document and manuscript storage box (*ch'aek bandaji*)
Paulownia wood, yellow brass fittings
Late nineteenth to early twentieth century, Kyŏngsang Province
H. 30.5, W. 60, D. 28.5 cm.

The small *bandaji*-type opening (without hinges here; the panel lifts out) is not often found on such boxes. The shape is similar to that of a wedding box.

135. Book storage *bandaji* (*ch'aek bandaji*)
Zelkova wood, iron fittings
Nineteenth century, Kyŏngsang Province.
H. 51, W. 87.5, D. 38.5 cm.

136. Book and manuscript storage
  bandaji (*ch'aek bandaji*)
Pine wood, iron fittings
Early nineteenth century, South
  Kyŏngsang Province
H. 40.5, W. 77, D. 35.5 cm.

This chest has a horizontal partition
inside just at the hinge level. The drawer
below can be removed for access to the
space below the partition. Such "hidden"
compartments are not uncommon, difficult access serving the same function as
a lock.

137. Book storage *bandaji* (*ch'aek bandaji*)
Zelkova wood, iron fittings, oil finish
Early nineteenth century, Ch'ungch'ŏng
  Province
H. 68.5, W. 101, D. 44.5 cm.

The drawers on this piece are unusual.
Drawers on *bandaji*, when and if they are
present, are generally small and on the
inside of the chest (but see the Yŏng-gwang
bandaji, Plate 33).

138. Chŏnju book storage chest (*Chŏnju bandaji*)
Pine wood, iron fittings, thick oil finish
Late nineteenth to early twentieth century, Chŏnju city area, North Chŏlla Province
H. 99, W. 94, D. 39.5 cm.

The wood of this chest is a hard pine without any "pretty" features. In fact, there is a large flaw on the top, which has been but roughly and incompletely filled. However, the total artlessness and forthright, square honesty of this piece is very appealing. The first impulse was to classify this as a clothes chest, but the shape of the lower opening argues against this use. Still, the piece shows none of the refinements associated with book chests and with the taste of the income group that could afford to buy and store books. Its use remains a matter of conjecture.

139. Chŏnju book storage chest (*kae-kumong bandaji* or *Chŏnju bandaji*)
Pine wood except for large central door of zelkova, iron fittings, oil finish
Early nineteenth century, Chŏnju city area, North Chŏlla Province
H. 96.5, W. 88.5, D. 39.5 cm.

The Chŏnju chest is characterized by two openings, with the larger one below. The door to the larger opening is of zelkova, which creates an interesting contrast with the pine wood construction of this simple country chest. The literal meaning of *kae-kumong* is a low gate or wall opening for a dog to come and go freely, an allusion to the low *bandaji*-style opening in such chests.

140. Two-level book and manuscript chest (*ich'ŭng ch'aekchang*)
Painted and cut paper on pine wood, oil finish
Middle nineteenth century, Kyŏngsang Province
H. 101, W. 98, D. 43.5 cm.
Collection: Mr. Nam Goong

Paper lends itself to a wide variety of decorative treatments. Here the upper and lower doors are painted, the former with butterflies, the latter with rocks and plants, while cut paper patterns are seen at the sides and center of the chest. The upturned ends of the top signify that this chest was for books and manuscripts.

141. Long stationery and book chest (*chang mungap*)
Pine wood, yellow brass fittings, oil finish
Middle nineteenth century, Kyŏnggi Province
H. 36.2, W. 144, D. 22 cm.
Collection: National Museum of Korea

This low cabinet for the gentleman-scholar has an exceptional shape and style—it is a unique piece. Its drawers are convenient for someone seated on the floor, and the niches and top provide places to display objects as well as to stack books.

142. Inkstone box (yŏnsang)
Paulownia wood, oil finish
Middle nineteenth century, Ch'ungch'ŏng Province
H. 26.7, W. 32.8, D. 20 cm.
Collection: Mr. Han Ki-taek

The craftsman knew precisely what he wanted when he made this charming and eccentric box. He cut his wood to dramatize the swirls and curls of the grain, then abraded away the softer wood to bring the grain into relief. In fact, this box appears to have been cut and hollowed out of a single piece of wood rather than to have been joined. Such pieces were favored by men of a literary or artistic bent.

143. Inkstone box (yŏnsang)
Ginkgo wood, oil finish
Middle nineteenth century, Naju city, South
   Chŏlla Province
H. 25.5, W. 42.5, D. 29.5 cm.

This form is a typical inkstone, brush, and stationery box; the two top panels are lids to compartments holding inkstone and brushes. The drawer is for paper and incidentals. Elaborate carvings depict a floral scroll pattern on the sides and cranes and clouds on the lids.

144. Inkstone box (yŏnsang)
Persimmon wood box, paulownia wood
   base, oil finish
Late nineteenth to early twentieth century,
   Seoul
H. 29, W. 40.5, D. 28.5 cm.
Collection: Mrs. Pongsoon Lee

This combination of hard and soft woods in an inkstone box of this kind is unusual.

145. Storage box and table for the Korean game of *paduk* (*paduk p'an*)
Ginkgo wood panels and top, pearwood frame and molding, oil finish
Late nineteenth century, Kyŏnggi Province
H. 33.3, W. 42.5, D. 42.5 cm.
Collection: National Museum of Korea

The inscriptions on the front panels refer to a man of resolution and heroic character.

146. Inkstone and stationery box (*yŏnsang*)
Ginkgo wood, zelkova frames on panels, yellow brass fittings, oil finish
Late nineteenth century, provenance uncertain
H. 29.6, W. 48.5, D. 33.2 cm.

The subtle proportions of this elegant box are nearly impossible to photograph. There is almost a monumental or architectural quality about it—it seems to have no size, or perhaps it could be gigantic or tiny with equal success. The doors on the bottom open in the same way as the document chest (*mungap*) in Plate 60, an unusual feature when combined with the conventional inkstone box arrangement of the top.

147. Letter holder (*pyŏnji-goji* or *kobi*)
Ginkgo wood, oil finish
Nineteenth century, Kyŏnggi Province
H. 52, W. 13, D. 6.3 cm.
Collection: Ewha Womans University Museum

This letter holder displays auspicious motifs meticulously carved against a background openwork fret pattern incorporating the Buddhist swastika.

148. Letter holder (*pyŏnji-goji* or *kobi*)
Paulownia wood
Late nineteenth to early twentieth century, Kyŏnggi Province
H. 81, W. 14, D. 13 cm.
Collection: Mr. and Mrs. Yoong Bae

Such letter holders are made to be hung on a wall.

149. Scholar's desk (*ch'aeksang* or *sŏan*)
Ginkgo wood, yellow brass fittings
Early twentieth century, Ch'ungch'ŏng
   Province
H. 25, W. 60, D. 29 cm.
Collection: Mr. and Mrs. Yoong Bae

The size, shape, and arrangement of metalwork
make this an exemplary piece of its kind.

150. Altar stands (*hyangno-sang*)
Pine wood, iron fittings
Middle nineteenth century, Ch'ungch'ŏng or Kyŏnggi Province
Left: H. 28.5, W. 56, D. 27.5 cm.
Right: H. 24.5, W. 43.5, D. 27.5 cm.

These stands or tables were used on simple family altars for ancestor worship. The door
in the piece on the right is a panel that pulls up through a slot in the top, a most unique
and unusual feature. Totally unprepossessing and simple, these little pieces have great
appeal and charm.

151. Scholar's desk (*ch'aeksang* or *sŏan*)
Pearwood, yellow brass fittings, oil finish
Middle nineteenth century, South
   Ch'ungch'ŏng Province
H. 43, W. 65, D. 32.5 cm.

152. Scholar's desk (*ch'aeksang* or *sŏan*)
Pine wood, zelkova wood drawer, yellow brass fittings, oil finish
Late eighteenth to early nineteenth century, South Chŏlla Province
H. 30.5, W. 61.5, D. 28 cm.

This little country desk epitomizes Yi dynasty furniture. It is natural and unpretentious, elegantly proportioned, imperfectly finished, intimate, and captivating.

MAP OF KOREA

Naju •

North Hamgyŏng

Yang-gang

Chagang

South Hamgyŏng

North P'yongan

South P'yongan

P'yŏngyang •

North
Hwanghae

Kangwŏn

South Hwanghae

Kaesŏng •

Kanghwa Island

• **Seoul**

Kangwŏn

Kyŏnggi

North
Ch'ungch'ŏng

South Ch'ungch'ŏng

Taejŏn •

North Kyŏngsang

• Chŏnju

• Taegu

North Chŏlla

South Kyŏngsang

Masan
•

• Kwangju

Pusan

South Chŏlla

Mokp'o •
• Yŏng-gwang

Cheju Island

0   100 km

To KNOW SOMETHING of the proper placement and use of furniture within a traditional Korean house is an important aspect of understanding the life-style of the Yi dynasty. The location of the house itself was considered significant for assuring the felicitous life of its occupants. Ideally it faced the south and had mountains to the north, water to the south, and trees all about. In a practical sense, this provided protection from the icy northern winds of winter, a sunny southern exposure, a scenic stream or pond for washing both body and clothes, and shade from the hot summer sun. In the Orient, rock, water, and wood are considered important elements for sustaining and supporting life; it was felt that the household should be encompassed by them, if not actually, at least symbolically or in a token sense.

A house was structured, in keeping with the strict tenets of Confucianism, so that men and women had separate living quarters. Confucianism, the Yi dynasty's underlying social philosophy, thus created a well-defined and somewhat austere living environment. In following the idea of separation of the sexes, the design of the upper-class Yi house provided inner rooms for the female quarters (*anch'ae*) and outer rooms for the male quarters (*sarang-ch'ae*). The servants' rooms were separated from the family quarters.

The men were usually served their meals separately either in the inner room (*sarang-bang*) of the men's area or on an attached balcony or veranda. After the men had eaten, women ate in their own inner room (*anbang*) or in the kitchen. Children seldom ate with adults. In general, a woman's status was strictly inferior to that of a man. The young wife was expected to wait upon her in-laws hand and foot and to obey her husband as she had obeyed her father. The strict separation of the sexes meant that the husband almost literally had to sneak into his wife's quarters under cover of dark. They were not supposed to have any direct encounter in the daytime. When a woman left the household, she was carried in a palanquin or sedan chair if she was of the upper class, or if she was of the middle or lower classes she was garbed from

THE TRADITIONAL KOREAN HOUSE AND ITS FURNITURE

head to toe with only holes for the eyes and nose. So a woman's kingdom or universe was the *anch'ae*, and within those confines she had a great deal of authority in supervising the daily routines of the household.

The rooms of the house were heated from beneath the stone and clay floors. A fire was made with kindling on one side of the outer part of the house, with a flue running the entire width of a room so that the smoke and heat would be drawn across and beneath the room. Oiled paper was laid on top of the clay floor, all corners and edges carefully sealed to prevent carbon monoxide from leaking into the house. Thus, the lower portion of a room was well heated, while the upper portion had less heat. This heating system (in Korean called *ondol*) fits in with the fact that basic life activities in the home took place on or near the floor. Pillows and cushions for sitting and mattress pads for sleeping were simply placed directly on the floor without chairs or bedframes. The low height of much of the furniture reflects this living style; furniture generally was made to be accessible to a person sitting or sleeping on the floor (Figure 23). Exceptions are two- and three-level clothing chests and kitchen furniture. The kitchen floor was unheated and usually simply of packed dirt.

The style, design, and size of a house were all carefully dictated by custom according to social position. The houses of the upper, middle, and lower classes were easily distinguishable from one another. By the end of the Yi dynasty, however, distinctions between the upper and middle classes had softened and rules relaxed so that there was much deviation from the original strict building dictates. However, the life-style described in this book was not something the lower classes would have had a chance to experience.

Figure 1 is a prime example of the floor-plan of a luxurious upper-class home of the middle to late Yi dynasty. This house, called the Yŏng Kyŏng-dang, was built and used by King Suncho in 1828. After he had been king for twenty-eight years, Suncho wanted to try living in an "ordinary" house to see whether or not a king could live in the kind of house inhabited by his subjects. Located on the Kyŏngbuk Palace grounds in Seoul, the Yŏng Kyŏng-dang was an upper-class (*yangban*) house of ninety-nine *kan*. At that time a *yangban* house could not legally be larger than one hundred *kan*. (One *kan* is variously defined as 210 square centimeters, 240 square centimeters, or 270 square centimeters). As seen in the diagram, the men's area is on the right and the women's on the left. The gatekeeper's and servants' quarters, the storage room, and the manger or barn were on either side of the large central gate through which all had to pass who came to the house.

Fig. 1. Floor plan of a Yi dynasty upper-class home

1. Women's quarters (*anch'ae*)
2. Men's quarters (*sarang-ch'ae*)
3. Women's inner room (*anbang*)
4. Side room for sleeping in the women's quarters, often used for children (*kŏnnŏbang*)
5. Master's room (*sarang-bang*)
6. Sleeping room in the men's quarters (*chimbang*)
7. Wooden-floored covered veranda (*rumaru*)
8. Open-aired pavilion for men's relaxation and entertaining

9. Main gate (*changnak mun*)
10. Servants' room (*pang*)
11. Storerooms (*kwang*)
12. Stable (*magutkan*)
13. Storeroom for palanquin or sedan chair (*kamabang*)
14. Entrance courtyard (*haengrangmadang*)
15. Gate from courtyard to women's area (*chein mun*)
16. Gate from courtyard to men's area (*changnak mun*)
17. Men's study area (*sonhyangche*)

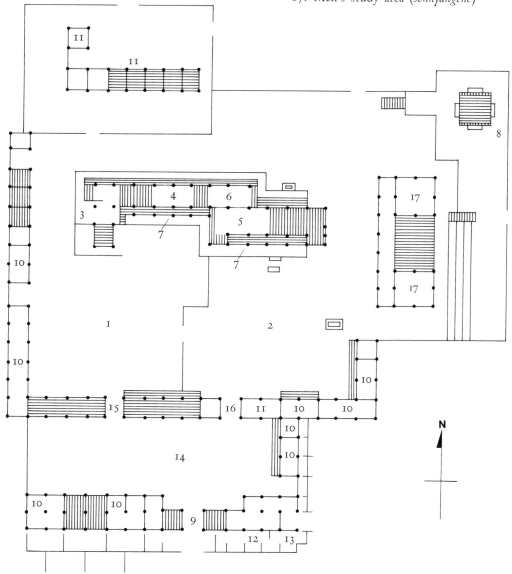

THE MEN'S QUARTERS (*sarang-ch'ae*)

As seen in Figure 1, the entrance to the men's quarters was across the courtyard from the main gate. This area could be one or two rooms, depending on a family's wealth or status. An elaborate men's area included an inner room with *ondol* heating, a wooden-floored veranda in front and to the side, and a private yard or garden. It also might have included an open-air pavilion for relaxing or entertaining in warm weather. The principal room of the *sarang-ch'ae* was called the *sarang-bang* (*bang* literally means "room"). The upper-class men's quarters also often included an adjoining wooden-floored room called the *rumaru*.

The *sarang-ch'ae* provided a place where the male owner of the house could do his reading, writing, and calligraphy; meditate; compose poems; receive guests; entertain friends and discuss various and sundry elevated subjects ranging from politics to philosophy to the arts. One can imagine the master of the household reigning over an evening session with his friends. He was normally stationed behind his small desk or table, legs crossed on the warm floor. Brushes, ink, inkstone, and paper were close at hand. Between cups of rice wine the guests would compose poems in a traditional verse style. Their work was expected to be of a high calligraphic standard as well as acceptable as poetry. Women servants would keep the guests supplied with snacks and drink brought from the kitchen on individual serving tables (*soban*). At some of these sessions, professional female entertainers (*kisaeng*) were brought in: highly trained and talented, they performed the traditional performing arts of dance and song and were dressed in the brightly colored traditional Korean women's dress (*ch'ima-chŏgori*). They performed on musical instruments, which might include the *kŏmungo*, a long six-stringed "zither" of paulownia wood with a back-piece of chestnut, or the *kayagŭm*, another "zither" of hollowed-out paulownia wood with twelve strings. The latter dates back at least to the sixth century and is related to the Chinese *zheng* and the Japanese *koto*. The *kŏmungo* is more uniquely Korean and is considered the most honored of Korean instruments, having a status comparable to that of the *qin* in China. Both instruments were played sitting cross-legged on the floor.

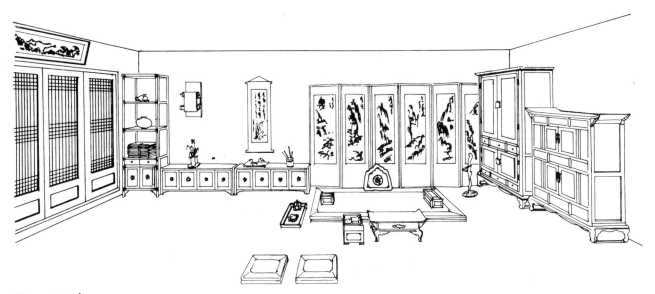

Fig. 2. Man's room

Aesthetic pursuits—philosophizing, artistic and literary creativity, and refined revelry —were what the Yi dynasty gentry used to entertain and relax.

Furnishings in the *sarang-bang* included mats and cushions; a small desk; one or a pair of stationery and incidentals boxes (*mungap*); book shelves; supplies needed for calligraphy; and a display stand (*sabang t'akja*) on which to stack books and scrolls and to display plants, ceramics, fans, curios, and miscellaneous objects. The furniture in the men's area was relatively simple, being mostly of wood adorned only by metal handles and hinges. In addition there were clothing chests; a Korean *go* set (a game known in Korean as *paduk*); and one or more musical instruments, as mentioned above. In the wooden-floored *rumaru*, used for sleeping and entertaining, was a bamboo mat and wooden bed, as well as other pieces. Paulownia and pine, woods with relatively subdued grains, were popular for *sarang-bang* furniture.

The Master's Room (*sarang-bang*)

In the reconstructed house on display at the Korean National Folk Art Museum a mannekin representing the master of the house sits before a scholar's desk with elaborately carved legs. On the left is a box for inkstone and writing implements. Against the right wall are a pair of stationery chests (*mungap*); a four-level book storage and display stand (*sabang t'akja*); and an enclosed book storage chest. The arrangement of this room is similar to but not quite the same as the example shown in Figures 2 and 3.

In the adjoining *rumaru* are a traditional bed, a book storage cabinet, and a work-stand with an armrest to the side. The bed is of the type used principally in the summer, with wooden or bamboo slats.

Fig. 3. Typical arrangement of furniture in a man's room

1. Book and display stand (*sabang-t'akja*)
2. Stationery and incidentals boxes (pair) (*mungap*)
3. Large cushion (*poryo*)
4, 5. Armrests
6. Inkstone box (*yŏnsang*)
7. Scholar's desk (*kyŏngsang*)
8. Oil lamp (*dung ch'ot* or *ch'ot-dae*)
9. Book chest (*ch'aekchang*)
10. Wardrobe chest (*ŭigŏri*)
11. Back rest (*ansŏk*)
12. Screen (*pyŏng-p'ung*)
13. Cushions
14. Storage chest (*chang* (not shown in drawing)
15. Ashtray

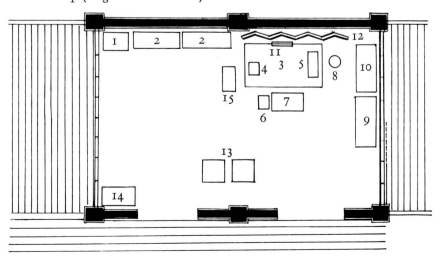

THE WOMEN'S QUARTERS (anch'ae)

In Figure 1, the women's quarters, sometimes referred to as the "happiest place in the house," is to the left of the main gate across the courtyard. No males other than members of the household or, occasionally, callers from the wife's family, were allowed into this area, where the women did their work and where all the materials they needed for working and living were kept. The main heated floor room, the *anbang*, often had a small room attached to it in which the family treasures were kept in chests. This *anbang*, literally meaning "inner room," was normally entered from a wooden-floored open porch (*taech'ung-maru*), which was used mainly in warm weather. Opposite the women's inner room and also off the porch area was a smaller sitting and sleeping room (*kŏnnŏbang*). The *anbang* itself, primarily for the master of the house and his wife, contrasts with the men's quarters in its more elaborate use of color and decoration. On the warmest part of the floor in the inner women's room near the kitchen—a space called the *arae-mok* in Korean—was placed a thick and colorful mat on which the woman of the house would sit and do her work or rest during the day. In front of this mat was a sewing box and a pot for a charcoal fire. On the opposite side of the room were chests for storage of clothes; a chest primarily for traditional white socks (*pŏsŏn*); a mirror box; low storage chests for stationery and incidentals (*mungap*); and one or a pair of wedding boxes (*ham*). Behind the sitting and working area usually could be found a painted (or embroidered) screen.

Woods used for furniture in the women's quarters, such as zelkova and persimmon, usually had decorative grains. There might also be chests and boxes decorated with painted ox horn panels; mother-of-pearl inlay; carving; incised brass fittings; and red or black lacquer. Decorative motifs included flowers; butterflies; birds; bats; Chinese characters for happiness and long life; symbols of longevity; the Buddhist swastika design; and fret patterns, among others (see pages 155-59).

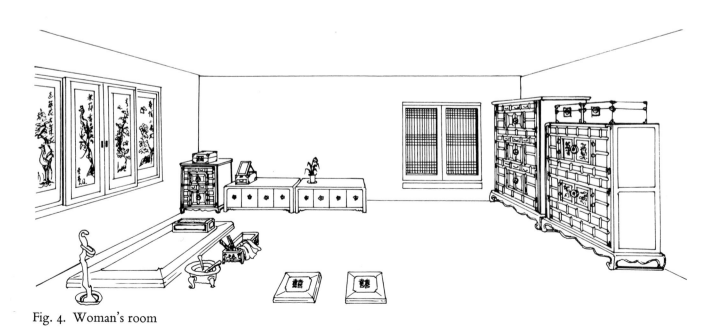

Fig. 4. Woman's room

The Women's Inner Room (*anbang*)

The *anbang* in the house reconstructed at the National Folk Art Museum in Seoul shows a seated female mannequin working behind a box for sewing implements. To the left, facing the figure, is a brass container for hot coals to provide additional heat—in effect, a hand-warmer. The stand to the right is an oil lamp. In the right corner is a two-unit stacked chest (*ich'ŭng nong*) for clothing storage. On the top of this is a mirror box with drawers for makeup and incidentals. Next is a low jewelry and incidentals box. There is a space between the latter and another low box, which is for an inkstone and brushes. Barely showing behind the large chest is a work stand, or scholar's desk, for reading and writing. The tall two-level chest (*ich'ŭng jang*) is also for clothing. On top of the this chest is a wedding box (*ham*), which contains mementos of the wedding festivities and is given by the groom to the bride.

Fig. 5. Typical arrangement of furniture in a woman's room
1. Low storage chest (this can be a *mŏrijang*, or headside chest; an *egijang*, meaning a baby or small-sized chest; or a *pŏsŏnjang*, a storage chest for padded socks).
2. Stationery and incidentals chests, pair (*mungap*)
3. Three-level clothing chest (*samch'ŭng jang*)
4. Two-unit stacked clothing storage chest (*ich'ŭng nong*)
5. Cushion (*poryo*)
6. Armrest
7. Storage chest (*bandaji* or *t'akja-jang*) (not shown in drawing)
8. Oil lamp (*dung ch'ot* or *ch'ot dae*)
9. Small cushions
10. Sewing box
11. Charcoal brazier
12. Mirror box (*kyŏngdae*)
13. Wedding boxes, pair (*ham*)
14. Document box (*sŏryu ham* or *sŏryu koi*)

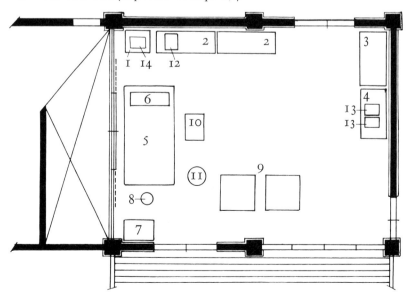

THE KITCHEN (*puŏk*)

The kitchen was usually connected to the women's inner room by a storage area called the *tarak-bang*. Found at a lower level than the women's inner room, the kitchen normally had a dirt floor and contained a cookstove as well as storage space for heavy cooking pots and other implements. In a small separate structure behind the women's area were storage rooms for supplies, food, and other materials; this structure also provided quarters for women servants. Behind the house there often could be found a small enclosed shrine for ancestor worship.

A typical kitchen arrangement of an upper-class house can be seen in Figures 6 and 7. Here a wooden-floored veranda open on the front adjoins the kitchen.

In Figure 7, the cooking area is on the left, and shelves and storage area on the right. In the right corner is a two-level kitchen cabinet, the bottom part of which is enclosed and the upper part open. On the large shelf in the upper right-hand corner are serving trays stacked upside down.

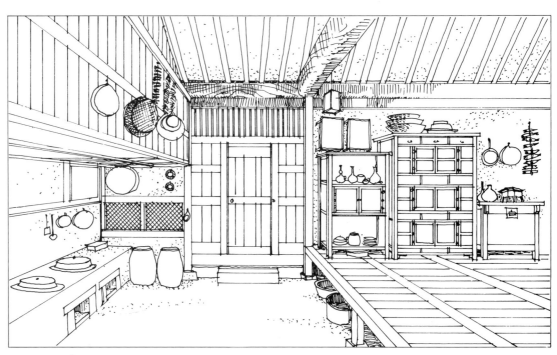

Fig. 6. Kitchen

Fig. 7. Kitchen

Fig. 8. Storage room adjoining kitchen

Adjoining the kitchen (Figure 8) is a storage room containing serving trays and dishes, and, in this instance, a grain storage box, which is partially visible next to the door. A four-level cabinet for dish and bottle storage is seen in the corner.

VERANDA (*taech'ung-maru*)

This area is a wooden-floored veranda under the roof of the house but open on the front. Here all sexes and ages could meet. It is next to the *anbang*, or women's inner room. An elaborately decorated two-level clothing chest is just inside the entrance to the *anbang*. At the far right is a rice storage chest (*ssal tuiju*).

Fig. 9. Veranda

In contrast to the upper-class house described above, in middle- and lower-class houses rooms were under one roof. There were differences from province to province, since houses were built to conform to environmental conditions such as temperature, building materials available, and living habits. For instance, there were some essential differences between town houses and mountain and farm houses. The farmhouse had sheds for farming equipment and a large level area outside the yard and gate of the house for threshing grain and related work. In the town this was impossible, because the street outside the house was public property; there the yard had to accommodate all work, including the threshing and drying of grain and the preparation of *kimchi*—the spicy cabbage and radish pickle essential to the Korean diet. In households of all social classes, pottery *kimchi* jars were stored in the yard or buried there during the period of pickling. The ordinary house in Seoul was L-shaped or U-shaped in order to provide maximum exterior working space. A wall of dried mud or stone (or a mixture) usually enclosed the property.

Because of severe winters and heating problems, houses in the northern part of the peninsula had no room or veranda with a wooden floor but instead often had an extra *ondol*-heated room. However, most houses in Seoul and south of Seoul usually had a central wooden-floored veranda open on the front for warm-weather use.

Most houses were constructed of wattle and daub and had thatched roofs. Outside doors usually were hung on iron hinges, while inside doors were in sliding grooves.

1. room   4. kitchen extension and work area
2. kitchen   5. veranda
3. storeroom

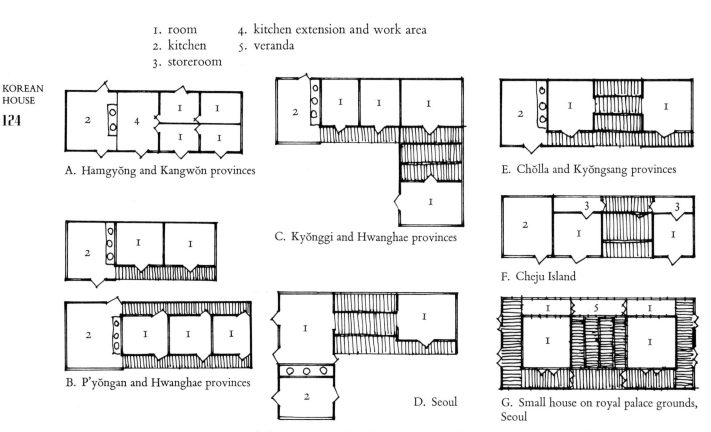

KOREAN HOUSE

124

A. Hamgyŏng and Kangwŏn provinces

B. P'yŏngan and Hwanghae provinces

C. Kyŏnggi and Hwanghae provinces

D. Seoul

E. Chŏlla and Kyŏngsang provinces

F. Cheju Island

G. Small house on royal palace grounds, Seoul

Fig. 10. Typical house plans of different regions (lined areas are unheated wooden-floored porches, verandas, and passageways)

Doors and windows were commonly paper on wooden frames, which often displayed decorative fret patterns. Windows were high in order to avoid drafts in the lower part of the room. In less affluent households, furniture was usually limited to one or two chests, small individual dining tables, and a small scholar's writing desk with drawers for writing implements and ink.

TYPES AND STYLES

Basic styles and shapes of Yi dynasty furniture were largely the same throughout the peninsula. Regional variations did exist, however, as reflected in differences in metalwork and, sometimes, proportions. Some of these differences are mentioned in discussion of individual styles below and in the plate captions.

The most widely used type of chest was the *bandaji* (see Plates 28–37). Virtually every Korean family had at least one. What characterizes the *bandaji* is its door, which usually extends all the way across the front and opens downward, with hinges located at about three-fifths the height of the front, though the hinge position varies considerably. Most *bandaji* are for clothing storage, though some are for books and manuscripts. Korean antique dealers call a *bandaji* a "blanket chest" in English, a term that seems to be gaining increasing usage among Westerners. There is no linguistic basis for this, however. The word *bandaji* means "half" (*ban* or *pan*) "closing" (*taji* or *-daji*). The term "blanket chest" possibly came about because in many middle- and lower-class households floor sleeping mats (*yo*) were folded and stacked on top of the *bandaji* during the daytime. For whatever reasons, this term undoubtedly started as a simple and easily understood way for dealers to refer to *bandaji* in English; it has nothing to do with traditional Korean terminology.

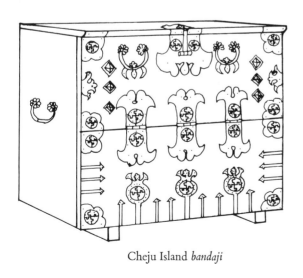

Cheju Island *bandaji*

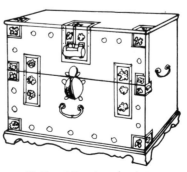

Kyŏnggi Province *bandaji*

Chŏnju chest

Fig. 11. *Bandaji*

The most common *bandaji* shape is seen in Plate 35, which shows a *bandaji* from Cheju Island, the large island off the south coast of the peninsula. The metalwork is characteristic of Cheju pieces, though sometimes similar ornamentation can be seen on pieces in the nearby southwestern coastal region of South Chŏlla Province. A similar shape, but with different metalwork, is seen in *bandaji* from Kyŏnggi Province, the area surrounding the capital city of Seoul (see Plate 28). The Kyŏnggi *bandaji* is especially prized among collectors, mainly because of its identification with the capital and the upper classes. A regional *bandaji* of a large size and with a distinct style of metalwork is shown in Plate 1; this is an upper-class *bandaji* from South Chŏlla. Another, quite different shape is seen in Plate 34; this is popularly known as a Chŏnju chest or Chŏnju *bandaji* after the city in North Chŏlla Province. Built on two levels within a single frame, only the lower section has a *bandaji*-type opening, while the top has double doors. On many Chŏnju chests small drawers are found at the top.

The Yŏng-gwang *bandaji* (Plates 3, 33) is still another regional variation, identified with a locality in South Chŏlla Province. It is taller than the Cheju or Kyŏnggi *bandaji* and has a smaller opening, which does not extend all the way across the front. The northern part of the peninsula has the Pyŏngyang *bandaji*, with elaborate brass-work (Plates 4, 32) and the *ssung-ssung-i bandaji*, with intricate, lacelike fittings of punched or wrought iron (Plate 31).

Another popular kind of storage chest is the *chang*, which has one or more compartments in a single vertical structure. The word *chang* literally means "chest" and becomes *-jang* in pronunciation when it is preceded by a descriptive or modifying syllable or syllables.

The *mŏrijang*, or "headside" chest (Plates 11-14, 46-48), is a single-level piece for the women's quarters; it is placed near the large sitting and sleeping mat and contains items frequently needed by the woman of the house, such as nightclothes. One rarely seen variety contains two compartments, one for the husband to use on his visits to the wife's room. A *pŏsŏnjang* is a small chest for storing padded socks for women. Taller two- and three-level *chang* for clothing storage can be seen in Plates 5 and 6.

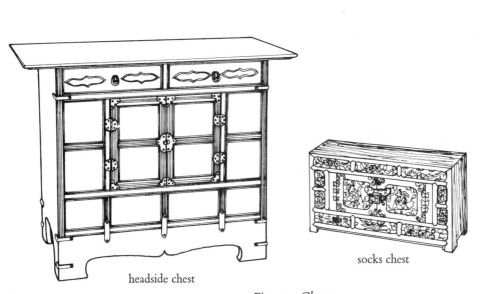

headside chest

socks chest

four-level chest

Fig. 12. *Chang*

Chang for book and document storage are distinguished by relatively subdued woods and fittings (Plates 128-30).

All types of *chang* have small doors opening out in the center of each level; each level is an empty compartment, without drawers or internal divisions. *Chang* are generally used for items that are frequently needed. There are often small drawers across the top of a *chang* and a decorative stand to keep it above the heated (*ondol*) floor.

three-level chest

book chest

kitchen chest

book chest

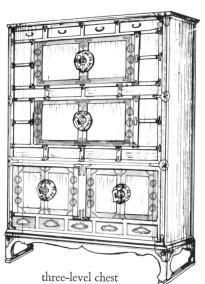

three-level chest

two-level chest

A wardrobe chest (*kwanbok-chang* or *ŭigŏri-jang*) has much larger doors than any other type of *chang*. It is usually composed of two compartments within a single frame (Plate 38), but occasionally may be constructed in two pieces (Plate 39), and it has a stand for raising it above the heated floor. The lower compartment is for folded clothing.

The distinction between a *nong*—another kind of storage cabinet—and a *chang* is not entirely clear. It is at least obvious, however, that the furniture referred to as *nong* (sometimes even called *chang nong*) is almost always composed of two identical or similar box units stacked on one another, usually, but not necessarily, with a stand (Plates 8–10, 40–45); a *chang*, on the other hand, is one or more compartments built within a single frame. The *nong* is generally referred to as an *ich'ŭng nong—i* means "two" and *ch'ŭng*, "level," "tier," or "story." The *nong* has double center doors on each level, considerably smaller than the front of the chest. A second distinction sometimes made between *nong* and *chang* is that the *chang* is for items used daily or at least frequently, while the *nong* is for long-term storage, for example, for seasonal clothing. This kind of distinction was probably observed more by upper-class families than by those of the middle and lower classes. Few lower-class families would have had a *nong* in any case.

Usually the two boxes composing the *nong* are identical, so they are interchangeable as top and bottom—the stand is removable in this case. Some *nong*, however, have a top distinguished by small drawers across the upper compartments. Sometimes, too, the stand is attached to one of the boxes, thus defining it as the lower compartment. Again, one box may have a finished top, while the other is unfinished, making it obvious which one goes on top. The *nong* chest is always a simple box form, never with a rim set off or top molding or frame that sticks out over the chest; this simple box structure is referred to as *ch'ŏnp'an* structure in Korean.

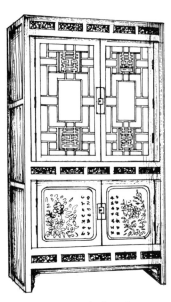

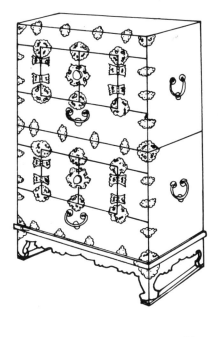

Fig. 13. Wardrobe chest

Fig. 14. *Nong*

Most wedding boxes (*ham* or *hon-su ham*) are low and wide (Plates 19, 20, 70–76). An exception is the Tongyang style, which is approximately cubical. The top part of a wedding box is the lid, which is hinged on the back and lifts up. Such boxes were not simply girls' "hope chests," but an integral part of the traditional wedding ritual. One or a pair of these boxes was transported to the home of the bride by a male friend of the groom on the eve of the wedding. The contents might include clothing, cloth, jewelry, silk thread, a cocoon and/or red paper—the last three are considered traditional symbols of fertility. In return, the bride's father usually would donate money to buy wine and food for the groom and his friends. The wedding box was taken to the bride's new home, where it was placed high on a two- or three-level chest—this was said to enhance the chances for success and high status for the groom and his family. Another and smaller type of wedding box (*saju t'anja ham*), hardly, if at all, distinguishable from a small document box, was used sometimes for the groom to transmit information to the bride's family concerning his birth date so as to determine the astrological compatibility of the prospective couple. The boards used to construct wedding boxes are rather thin and light in weight, the most popular wood being paulownia. Fittings are commonly yellow or white brass, but iron is seen as well. Regional styles exist, but these have not been systematically studied. A hint of the variety of wedding boxes can be seen in the photographs included here.

Women of the Yi dynasty, especially those of the aristocracy and royalty, also had various small boxes for storing valuables and incidentals such as jewelry, cosmetics, combs, hairpins, sewing materials, writing implements and the like (Plates 16–18, 63–69).

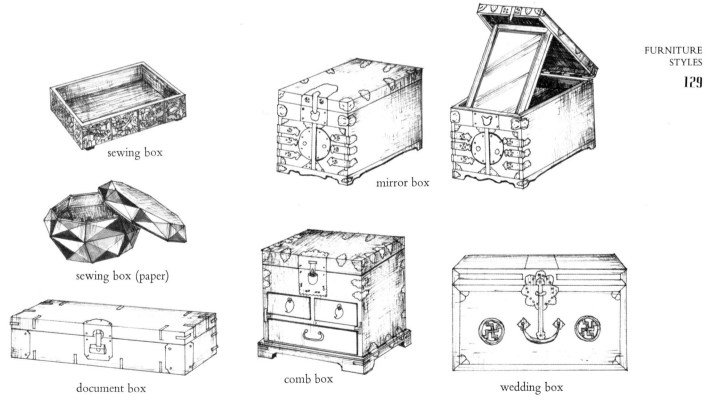

sewing box

mirror box

sewing box (paper)

document box

comb box

wedding box

Fig. 15. Boxes

There are two types of boxes for storing money and valuables—the coin chest and the "safe." The coin chest (*ton-kwe*) is a low, rectangular box with the front half or two-thirds of the top acting as a lid (Plates 23, 77–79). Sometimes the lid is hinged, but often not—in the latter case the lid can be removed completely. The box is locked on the front. The interior is empty space, without compartments, for holding the holed brass or copper coins in use during the Yi dynasty. These coins were strung together, since they were worth little individually—the sheer bulk of the accumulated coins required these large storage containers to protect the family's money. Fittings usually are iron.

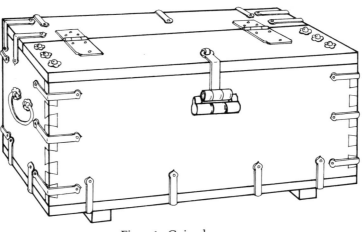

Fig. 16. Coin chest

The "safe" (*kap-kae suri*) for documents, money and other valuables is a small rectangular box with double doors covering nearly the entire front and with drawers taking up the interior space (Plates 21, 22). Metal fittings may be of brass or wrought iron. A keyhole lock secures the doors. The *kap-kae suri* is similar in appearance and structure to traditional Chinese medicine boxes of Ming dynasty styling and to nineteenth century Japanese boxes for storage of documents and valuables.

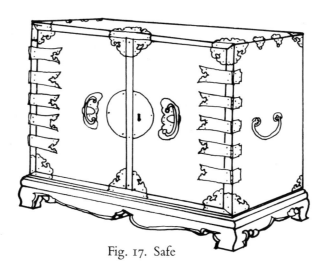

Fig. 17. Safe

The low, individual study table or desk is called a *sŏan* or *ch'aeksang* (Plates 149, 151, 152) or, in the case of the elaborate style associated with Buddhist studies and temples, a *kyŏngsang* (Plate 26). The Buddhist style of desk was sometimes used in private homes as well as in temples, and normally is identifiable by Buddhist swastika symbols carved on the side. Often, but not always, *sŏan* and *kyŏngsang* have upturned ends, a traditional touch that has the practical advantage of keeping writing materials and open scrolls from falling off the top (Plate 26). Offering tables for ancestor-worship altars are of similar shape and proportions to these scholar's desks, though sometimes a bit taller (Plate 150).

Fig. 18. Buddhist-style desk

A *mungap* is a low, rectangular chest for storage of stationery and writing materials, and sometimes valuables. Usually it is about the height of the scholar's desk. Some are drawered, but more often they have three or four front panels (called *pokp'an*) that lift up and out (Plates 15, 59, 60). The grooves holding these panels are constructed so that only one panel (usually the second from the right) can be lifted out—the others have to be slid to this same position to allow removal. Some versions have these panels and small interior top drawers as well. Others are completely open inside. *Mungap* were used by the Yi dynasty literati for storing paper, brushes, ink sticks, and inkstones for mixing ink, among others. *Mungap* could be found in both the men's and women's quarters.

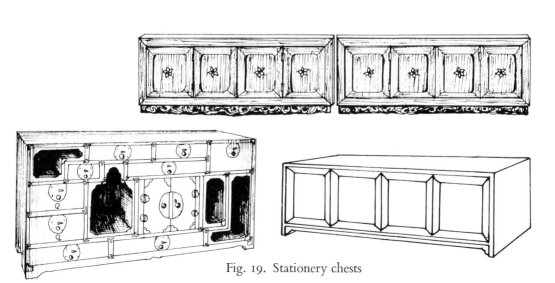

Fig. 19. Stationery chests

Open-shelved stands (*t'akja*) were normally placed next to one or a pair of *mungap* and were for displaying pottery and stacking books or manuscripts (Plates 122–125). They can be of two to five levels, with the bottom level usually enclosed and having double doors. There seems to be no rule about this, however: the enclosed levels vary, and rarely, all levels are enclosed (Plate 127). The doors for women's *t'akja* are most often of woods with decorative grain such as persimmon, maple, cherry, and zelkova. Men's *t'akja* are more likely to have bottom doors of subdued wood grain, such as paulownia. *T'akja* are usually made of three different woods—decorative panels for the doors, a hardwood for the frame, and paulownia for the shelves and sides. The back of an enclosed level might be of still another wood, most probably pine. Metal fittings are of brass or iron.

Fig. 20. Book and display stands

A final basic type to be mentioned is that of storage chests for rice (*ssal tuiju*) and dried beans (*p'at tuiju*) (Plates 86, 87). These were often kept on the front, wooden-floored veranda of the traditional Korean house. The basic shape is a box, but with straight legs lifting it fifteen centimeters or more off the floor. As with coin boxes, the front three-fifths to half of the top is the lid, which can be lifted off completely unless it is locked in front. These boxes are quite sturdy, with thick boards, usually pine, used for the frame. The front panel is ideally of a pleasing thick slice of zelkova, though pine is more often used. Lock and lock plate are iron.

Fig. 21. Rice storage chest

The detachable stands and the attached legs of chests display a surprisingly wide variety of styles, but generally the legs are cabriole and the stretchers between legs show profiles of complex curves.

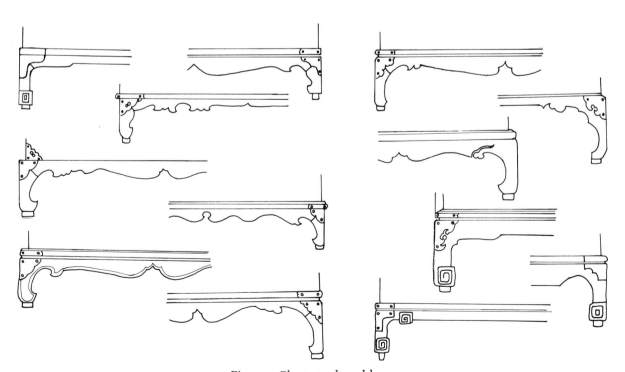

Fig. 22. Chest stands and legs

The accompanying drawing shows a variety of Korean furniture styles. Commonly accepted sizes are shown in relation to the average adult's height, considered to have been about 164 centimeters. The authority for this determination is unclear. As seen here most pieces have either attached or removable stands to keep them from direct contact with the traditional, heated (*ondol*) floors.

Fig. 23. Relative heights of furniture types

1. Three-tiered clothing chest (*samch'ŭng jang*)
2. Wardrobe chest (*kwanbok chang* or *ŭigŏri-jang*)
3. Open-shelved, four-level book and display stand with enclosed lower compartment (*sabang t'akja*)
4. Kitchen cabinet (*ch'an-jang*)
5. Two-level clothing chest (*ich'ŭng jang*)
6. Two-unit stacked clothing chest (*ich'ŭng nong*)
7. Three-level book storage chest (*samch'ŭng ch'aeksang*)
8. Enclosed, two-level storage chest (*ich'ŭng jang*)
9. Open-shelved, three-level display and storage stand with enclosed lower compartment (*sabang t'akja*)
10. Four-level women's padded socks storage chest (*sabang pŏsŏnjang*)
11. Two-level book storage chest (*ich'ŭng ch'aekchang*)
12. Enclosed *bandaji* clothing storage chest (*bandaji*)
13. Rice storage chest (*ssal tuiju*)
14. Single-level clothing storage chest—headside chest (*mŏrijang*)
15. Three-level women's storage chest for padded socks (*pŏsŏnjang*)
16. Safe with double doors (*kap-kae suri*)
17. Stationery and incidentals box (*mungap*)
18. Scholar's study table or desk (*sŏan* or *ch'aeksang*)
19. Buddhist-style scholar's study table or desk (*kyŏngsang*)
20. Dining or snack table (*soban*)
21. Mirror box (*kyŏngdae*)
22. Inkstone box (*yŏnsang*)

THE KOREAN PENINSULA has a wide variety of woods suitable for furniture construction. At least until the mid-nineteenth century, these woods grew in abundance and were more than sufficient for the needs of the relatively thinly populated nation. Nature has been kind in this regard, for Korea has a mountainous terrain and a plentiful water supply from its many streams and rivers. Seasonal differences are quite pronounced, and there is ample rainfall for support of vegetation and crops. The south is characterized by a temperate, mixed hardwood forest with some softwoods, and the north by mixed coniferous forests—that is, largely softwoods. By the late nineteenth century, however, many mountains and hills had become deforested because of the firewood needs of an increasing population. Even so, the supply of woods for furniture never seems to have reached a critically low level, at least judging by the large numbers of chests, tables, and boxes that were produced in the late nineteenth and early twentieth centuries.[1]

Hardwoods with decorative grains were much more plentiful in the southern half of the peninsula than in the north. Presumably for this reason, wood craftsmen and consumers in the south developed a taste for relatively unadorned cabinetry, usually avoiding excessive and ornate metalwork. In general, they tended to let the wood grain speak for itself. In the north, however, the woods in greater supply were those without decorative grains, a possible reason why much metalwork was placed on the facade; often brass was incised with traditional auspicious motifs or iron was punched with fine, lacelike openwork patterns (Plate 31). The more subdued pieces of southern origin are those most treasured by serious Korean collectors these days.

Woods widely used to provide decorative grains for front panels of furniture included zelkova, persimmon, maple, cherry, and Korean ash. Often they were cut thin and backed with pine or paulownia to provide added strength and to reduce the possibility of cracking.

The irresistible zelkova grain invited craftsmen to use it for practically every kind of chest. A single slab sliced in two vertically produces two panels whose grain

WOODS

patterns are mirror images. Such mirror-image panels were commonly used to provide a balanced composition on a chest front. When finished with oil or natural lacquer, zelkova has a glowing, slightly reddish appearance. Zelkova burl has a complex swirl pattern, perceived in Korea as coiled dragons—hence the name "dragon wood" (*yong-mok*; Plate 3). Korean ash also has an intricate, swirling grain pattern (Plate 55). Thick and wide zelkova boards were sometimes used for *bandaji* construction (Plates 35, 37). Zelkova, thick slices in particular, is not so prone to crack under fluctuating temperature conditions as some other hardwoods, especially persimmon. Even zelkova, however, will sometimes crack with changes in humidity.

Highly prized in Japan as well as in Korea, zelkova is known in the former country by the name *keyaki*. In Korea it is known as both *nŭtŭi namu* and *kwemok*. The elm (*nŭrŭp namu* in Korean) is of the same botanical family, *Ulmaceae*, and usually Korean antique dealers and tradesmen confuse the two. *Kwemok*—zelkova—is almost always identified as "elm" in English, though the overriding majority of pieces whose wood is called "elm" seem to be zelkova, a tree less well known in the West. The confusion is natural, since both trees have similar qualities of grain (though elm is usually less distinctive), density, and durability.

Persimmon (*kam namu*) is highly decorative, with the most popular variety for furniture construction having a spectacular dark grain figuration that contrasts dramatically with its light-colored background (Plates 16, 39). Seldom was an entire piece of furniture made of persimmon, but rather this wood was for decorative panels—often balanced mirror images—with woods of less dramatic grain used for the rest of the piece (see Plate 1 for a rare exception to this rule).

Maple (*tanp'ung namu*) has a somewhat orange tinge. Cherry (*pŏt namu*) has a blurred grain pattern and is darker than maple. Ordinarily cherry wood is stained.

The more decorative woods were used primarily for the women's quarters, but sometimes in the men's room as well. More common woods for men's pieces were pine (*so namu*) and paulownia (*odong namu*). These are relatively subdued and somber, in keeping with the decor expected of a gentleman-scholar's surroundings. Both are

Fig. 24. Zelkova

Fig. 25. Paulownia

softwoods, though some hard varieties of pine were used for chests. Paulownia is quite light in weight and heavily grained but without contrast in coloration; it is often treated with a hot iron in some manner and rubbed with straw or whatever to achieve a subdued finish and, at the same time, to make the grain stand out in relief (Plate 142). The same process is sometimes used on pine. Probably because it is lightweight and easy to lift or move about, paulownia was a popular wood for wedding boxes and the sides and backs (and often the fronts as well) of stacked chests for the women's rooms (see Plate 40 for a stacked chest entirely of paulownia). Paulownia is known for withstanding moisture and temperature changes and is considered to have insect-repellent qualities, like western cedar, so it is especially popular for pieces to store clothes, books, and manuscripts.

Korean furniture-makers talk about two types of pine—pine (*so namu*) and pine nut or piñon pine (*chat namu*). These trees grew abundantly throughout the peninsula, reaching maturity in relatively few years. These two have been dependable and plentiful sources of wood for Korean cabinetry, especially the former. All types of furniture are made of pine, a softwood with a clean but not particularly symmetrical grain; it is not as decorative as zelkova and persimmon, among others, when used for matching panels on a chest, but it is sometimes used in this manner, as seen in Plate 83. As mentioned above, pine and paulownia are both used as backing for thin paneling (not thin enough to be called a veneer) of the decorative woods.

Pearwood (*pae namu*) has the least clearly defined grain figure among the hardwoods used for furniture in Korea. Grown in the south, it is hard, sturdy, relatively crack resistant, and particularly useful as a frame material for large- and medium-sized chests. Sometimes it is used for part or all of small tables, women's incidentals, boxes, and desks, among others, and rarely for large pieces (see Plate 2 for an oversized *bandaji* constructed entirely of pearwood). Other than pear, woods valued for their hardness and strength in building frames for compartmentalized storage chests are walnut (*hodo namu*) and, in areas where available, red oak (*chamjuk namu* or *chamjung namu*). Red oak is found in Hwanghae and Chŏlla provinces.

Fig. 26. Pine

Fig. 27. Ginkgo

The favorite wood for making small serving tables (*soban*) is ginkgo (*ŭnhaeng namu*), a hardwood that has a fairly inconspicuous, crack resistant grain. Walnut is a prized wood for *soban* construction as well, but not nearly so widely used as ginkgo. Pine and piñon also are popular for this purpose. Zelkova provides an attractive pattern for *soban* tops, but is more likely to crack than ginkgo or walnut. Ginkgo is often used for wardrobe chests because of its reputation as being insect and moth repellent. Yet, paulownia, with the same reputation, is used primarily for stacked chests and wedding boxes as well as for wardrobe chests.

Limewood (*p'i namu*)—also called basswood and linden in the West—is a straight-grained softwood popular for *bandaji* construction, especially in the northern part of Korea, where woods with decorative grains are in short supply. Juniper (*hyang namu*) is another softwood—straight-grained and insect repellent—especially suitable for the inside drawers, shelves, and linings of wardrobe and clothing chests. Chestnut (*pam namu*), plentiful throughout the country, is a hardwood of undistinguished grain and has never been considered a prime material for cabinetry; because of its availability, however, it has been used especially by the lower classes for making simple pieces.

Small wooden pegs or dowel pins for joinery are most often made of bamboo, but sometimes of such hardwoods as birch (*pakdal namu*) and jujube, also called Chinese date (*taech'u namu*).

Open-shelved display and book storage stands, storage chests, and stacked chests were usually constructed of two, three, or even four kinds of wood: woods with decorative grain were used for front panels, strong hardwoods for frames, and pine or paulownia for sides and back (see Plates 125 and 126 for chests with three kinds of wood).

The following chart offers information about the terminology, provenance, and characteristics of a variety of Korean woods used in one way or another in furniture construction.

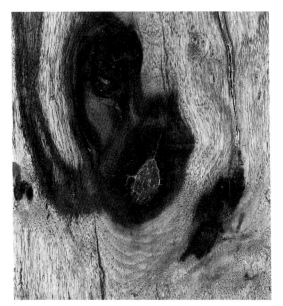

Fig. 28. Persimmon

Fig. 29. Pearwood

1. The situation in Korea contrasts with that in China, where available woods for furniture have been in short supply or inferior to those imported from Southeast Asia.

   Korea had a rich variety of woods, while China had to import prized hardwoods from the tropical regions to the south, particularly Indochina and the Malay regions. Most of these Chinese woods are known in the West as rosewood, but actually are various species of *Pterocarpus*. The four best known in China are *zitan* (*tzu-t'an*), *huali*, *hongmu* (*hung-mu*), and *jichimu* (*chi-ch'ih-mu*). Two of these, *huali* and *hongmu*, became popular in Korea, usually for recreating Chinese styles.

   Zitan has been identified by most experts as *Pterocarpus santalinus* and is found in the tropical forests of India and the Sunda Islands; another theory has it that it is *Dalbergia benthamii*, a closely related genus. Ecke suggests that both have been traded in China under the same name of *zitan*

   Huali is known in Korea as *hwa-ryu*. Ecke suggests that the most probable botanical name is *Pterocarpus indicus*, imported to China from Annam and Cambodia. A less desirable Chinese variety of this wood, but with similar characteristics, has the botanical identification of *Ormosia henryi*. It seems likely that some *hwa-ryu* imported into Korea might actually have been *Ormosia*.

   Hongmu literally means "red wood" and is known as *hong-mok* in Korean. Ecke says it has been identified as a subspecies of *Pterocarpus indicus* and that it was considered a less costly substitute for *huali*. *Hongmu* is grown in southern China and Southeast Asia.

   A fourth wood, *jichimu*, is more difficult to identify, according to Ecke. The earlier used Southeast Asian variety of this wood has been labeled as *Cassia siamea Lam*, while later pieces were often made from *Ormosia hosiei*, or the *hongdou* tree indigenous to central and western China.

   As indicated above, the two woods sometimes used in Korea were *hauli* (*hwa-ryu*) and *hongmu* (*hong-mok*), and the principal use seems to have been for furniture of Chinese design rather than for pieces of more distinctively Korean design. For an elaboration of the above, see Gustav Ecke, *Chinese Domestic Furniture* (Tokyo: Charles E. Tuttle Co., 1962).

The chart of Korean woods on pages 140–141 is a revised and expanded version of the chart in E. R. Wright, "A Note on Yi Dynasty Furniture Making," *Transactions* (Seoul: Royal Asiatic Society, Korea Branch, Vol. 52, 1977), pp. 39–44.

Fig. 30. Korean ash

PRINCIPAL KOREAN WOODS IN TRADITIONAL FURNITURE-MAKING

Name	Popular Korean Name	Genus and Species	Family	Properties	Geographic Distribution in Korea	Principal Use
pine	*so namu*	*Pinus densiflora* Siebold and Zuccarin	*Pinaceae*	Evergreen, needle-leafed, large-sized. Softwood.	All parts at most altitudes.	All kinds and parts of furniture.
zelkova	*nŭtŭi namu* or *kwe-mok*	*Zelkova serrata* (Thunberg) Makine	*Ulmaceae*	Deciduous, broad-leafed, large-sized. Hardwood.	Central and southern, altitudes of 50–1200 meters.	Principally for front panels, but all other parts as well. The veneer of the roots and burls (*yong-mok*) is also used for front panels.
paulownia	*odong namu*	*Paulownia coreana* Uyeki	*Paulowniaceae*	Deciduous, broad-leafed, large-sized. Softwood.	Central and southern, altitudes of 50–400 meters.	All parts. Especially for wedding boxes, book storage chests, and stacked chests.
persimmon	*kam namu*	*Diospyros kaki* Thunberg	*Ebenaceae Ventenat*	Deciduous, broad-leafed, large-sized. Softwood.	South, altitudes of 100–700 meters.	Usually for front panels.
pear	*pae namu*	*Pyrus serotina* Culta Rehd	*Pyrus*	Deciduous, broad-leafed, small-sized. Hardwood.	All parts.	Usually for frames. Sometimes for small boxes. Good for carving.
ginkgo	*ŭnhaeng namu*	*Ginkgo biloba* L.	*Salisburyaceae*	Deciduous, large-sized. Hardwood.	All parts, low altitudes to 500 meters.	All kinds, but especially for heavily used pieces such as serving tables, inkstone containers, bases for grain grinding vessels, and others. Good for carving.
birch	*pakdal namu*	*Betula schmidtii* Regel	*Retulaceae*	Deciduous, broad-leafed, large-sized. Hardwood.	All parts, altitudes of 300–2000 meters.	For small pieces such as laundry beaters and wooden pillows. Pegs or dowels for joinery.
white birch	*chajak namu*	*Betula japonica* Sieb	*Betulaceae*	Deciduous, broad-leafed, large-sized. Hardwood.	North, altitudes of 209–2100 meters.	Especially for frames. Sometimes front panels.
bamboo	*tae namu*	*Sasa spiculosa* Mak. and Shib. (W.)	*Bambusaceae*	Evergreen, thin-leafed, straight, usually small-sized. Hardwood.	Southern coastal areas, low altitudes	Sometimes in slats or strips for panels. Pegs or dowels for joinery. Beds.
walnut	*hodo namu*	*Juglans sinensis* Dode	*Juglandaceae Lindley*	Deciduous, large-leafed, large-sized. Hardwood.	Central and southern, altitudes of 50–400 meters.	Serving tables and frames.
jujube or Chinese date	*taech'u namu*	*Zizypfius jujuba* Miller	*Rhamnaceae Lindley*	Deciduous, small-leafed, large-sized. Hardwood.	All parts, altitudes of 100–500 meters.	Principally for frames, and pegs or dowels for joinery.

Name	Popular Korean Name	Genus and Species	Family	Properties	Geographic Distribution in Korea	Principal Use
pine nut (piñon)	*chat namu*	*Pinus koraiensis* Siebold and Zuccarin	*Pinaceae*	Evergreen, needle-leafed, large-sized. Softwood.	All parts, altitudes of 100–1900 meters.	All parts.
juniper	*hyang namu*	*Juniperu* Linne	*Juniperaceae*	Evergreen, needle-leafed, large-sized. Softwood.	All parts except P'yongan and Hamgyong, altitudes lower than 800 meters.	For all parts of wardrobe and clothing chests, but especially for inside drawers, shelves, and linings. Considered insect repellent.
chestnut	*pam namu*	*Castanea crenata*	*Fagaceae Prantl*	Deciduous, narrow-leafed, large-sized. Hardwood.	All parts, altitudes of 100–1100 meters.	For all kinds and parts of furniture. Popular with lower classes because of availability.
maple	*tanp'ung namu*	*Acer formosum* Carriere variety coreanum Nakai	*Aceraceae*	Deciduous, broad-leafed, large-sized. Hardwood.	All parts, altitudes of 100–1600 meters.	For front panels.
elm	*nŭrŭp namu*	*Ulmus davidiana* Planchon variety japonica Nakai	*Ulmaceae*	Deciduous, broad-leafed, large-sized, Hardwood.	All parts, altitudes of 100–1200 meters.	Sometimes for front panels and frames.
willow	*pŏdŭ namu*	*Salix koreensis*	*Salicaceae*	Deciduous, large-leafed, large-sized. Hardwood.	All parts, altitudes of 50–1300 meters.	Feeding troughs, wooden footwear, and others.
cherry	*pŏt namu*	*Prunus serrulata* Lindley	*Amygdalaceae Reichenbach*	Deciduous, large-leafed, large-sized.	All parts, altitudes of 100–1500 meters.	For front panels.
red sandalwood (also called "rosewood")	*hwaryu* or *chadan namu*	*Pterocarpus santalinus* L.	*Santalaceae*	Hardwood	Imported from Southeast Asia and China	For all parts, usually Chinese-style furniture. Used by upper classes.
red oak	*ch'amjuk* or *ch'amjung namu*	*Tooha sinensis* Roem or *Cedrela sinensis* Juss	*Meliaceae Ventenat*	Deciduous, broad-leafed, large-sized. Softwood.	Hwanghae and the Chŏlla at altitudes of 100–600 meters.	Especially for wardrobe chests and frames for display and book storage stands (*t'akja*). Good for carving.
lime or basswood or linden	*p'i namu*	*Tilia amurensis* Ruprecht variety barbegera Nakai and Kawamoto	*Tiliaceae Jussieu*	Deciduous, large-leafed, large-sized. Softwood.	All parts, altitudes of 100–1400 meters.	Furniture panels. Especially used in north for *bandaji*. Sometimes for serving tables.
Korean ash	*mulp'uri namu*	*Eunymus sieboldianus*	*Celastraceae*	Deciduous, large-sized. Hardwood.	All parts except Hwanghae and South P'yongan, altitudes of 500–1300 meters.	Especially front panels.

141

Most Yi dynasty joinery techniques in furniture construction can be described in general by several terms used in western cabinetry, though English-language woodworking and carpentry books and dictionaries often do not reveal an exact counterpart for a Korean technique and also present a confusing variety of terms for a single method or joint. Metal fittings were used both to decorate and to strengthen; metal nails were considered desirable only for attaching metal fittings to the wood. Fish or animal glue was often used, especially for small pieces and when the joinery was delicate or weak.

Top joinery. There are three types of top contruction for Yi dynasty chests and boxes. One is an overhanging board (*kaep'an* structure) that is larger than the body of the chest. This is seen, for example, in many but not all scholar's tables, some stationery chests, some safes, and many book storage chests (Plates 25, 130, 132, and 149). The most common joinery technique in this instance is mortise and tenon (*changbu ch'ŏk*).

A second kind of overhanging (*kaep'an*) structure has a frame built around the top panel. The top panel fits into a groove in the frame (tongue and groove technique, but this is given the same dictionary translation in Korean as mortise and tenon—*changbu ch'ŏk*). The four frame bars are joined at the edges with a mitre joint—those in Figures 31C, D and 31E are slip-feather mitre joints. This is the method normally used on two- or three-tiered storage chests (*chang*) and headside chests (*mŏrijang*) (see Plates 13, 48).

A third kind of top contruction (the *ch'ŏnp'an* structure) is a simple box with no overhanging top. Joinery is, variously, tongued mitre (*ragodoham*); half-lap (*yŏljang giŭm*); dovetail or finger joints (*sagae*); or mortise and tenon (*changbu ch'ŏk*) (Figure 32). These techniques have been most used with *bandaji*, stacked chests (*nong*), wedding boxes (*ham*), and sometimes small document and incidentals boxes of various sorts. The same word in Korean, *ragodoham*, is given as a dictionary definition of

JOINERY

both rabbet joint and mitre joint. Half-lap or rabbeting was most easily and often used with hardwoods such as pear, zelkova, and ginkgo. On less carefully made pieces, fewer mortise-and-tenon joints or half-lap joints were used.

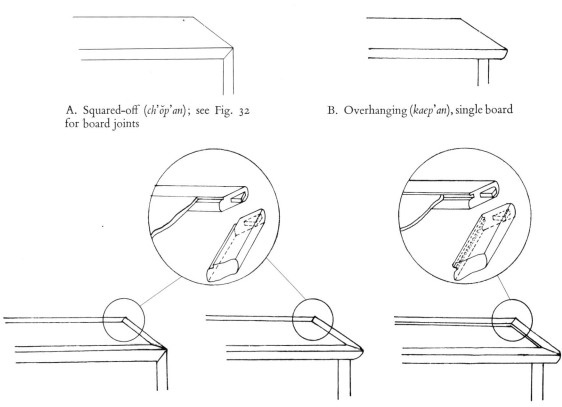

A. Squared-off (*ch'ŏp'an*); see Fig. 32 for board joints

B. Overhanging (*kaep'an*), single board

C. Squared-off (*ch'ŏp'an*), frame and panel

D. Overhanging (*kaep'an*), frame and panel. In both (C) and (D) the frame has slip-feather mitre joints and the panel is fitted into the frame with a lap joint and is glued. Frame and panel surfaces often are flush.

E. Overhanging (*kaep'an*), frame and recessed panel. Panel is fitted into frame with tongue-and-groove joint and may be glued or floating.

Fig. 31. Structures of chest tops

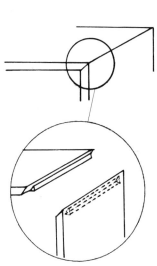

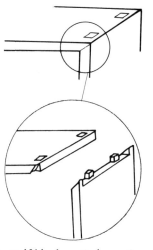

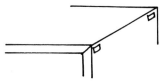

C. Half-blind horizontal mortise and tenon

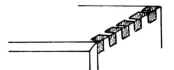

D. Finger joints or dovetails

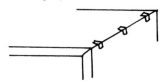

A. Full-blind tongued mitre joint

B. Half-blind vertical mortise and tenon

E. Mock finger joints

Fig. 32. Carcase joinery for squared-off structure (*ch'ŏp'an*) of chest top

Small scholar's tables or desks often have upturned ends, which are either rabbeted and glued or fitted with half-laps and glued (see Figure 33).

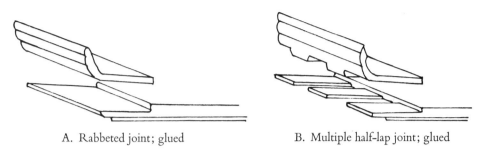

A. Rabbeted joint; glued   B. Multiple half-lap joint; glued

Fig. 33. Upturned ends of scholar's desk

With heavy furniture such as coin boxes (*ton-kwe*) and *bandaji*, metal staples or braces are often used on top and side panels (see Plates 77, 138).

Side panel joinery. Side panels commonly are joined by half-lap or rabbeting. Metal fittings are often wrapped around corners and fastened with metal nails, providing strength as well as ornamentation (see Plates 21, 23).

Door structure. The doors on chests (*chang*) and stacked box chests (*nong*) usually have frames with inset panels. Door frames generally display slip-feather mitre joints. Door panels are inset into the door frames by tongue and groove, sometimes with added strengthening by glue (see Figures 31C, D, E and 34). Such door panels are often constructed of a thin slice of precious wood backed by woods with less decorative grain such as pine or paulownia, thereby minimizing the likelihood of cracking when temperature and moisture fluctuated and also permitting flexible use of decorative wood grains, such as with mirror image panels. On some elaborate chests for the women's quarters, narrow strips of wood are inlaid around the edges of doors and panels (see Plate 46).

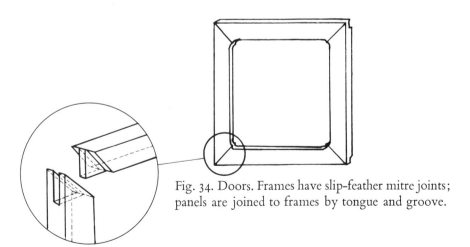

Fig. 34. Doors. Frames have slip-feather mitre joints; panels are joined to frames by tongue and groove.

Molding for front panels. Molding bars were used to separate front panels on chests, permitting greater flexibility in design. For example, in using relatively small panels, it was easier for the Korean cabinetmaker to make the popular balanced, mirror-image composition.

Three ways for joining or fitting molding bars to one another are illustrated in Figure 35: one is pointed and fitted into the crossbars; one is squared and flush against the crossbars; and one is squared and fitted into the crossbars. The short vertical molding bars are generally attached with glue and are known to pop out under changing temperature and moisture conditions. The top horizontal rail is generally joined at the corners by mitre and half-lap joinery. The lower horizontal strips may be joined by mortise and tenon or simply fitted and glued. Cross-sections of molding bars are shown in Figure 36.

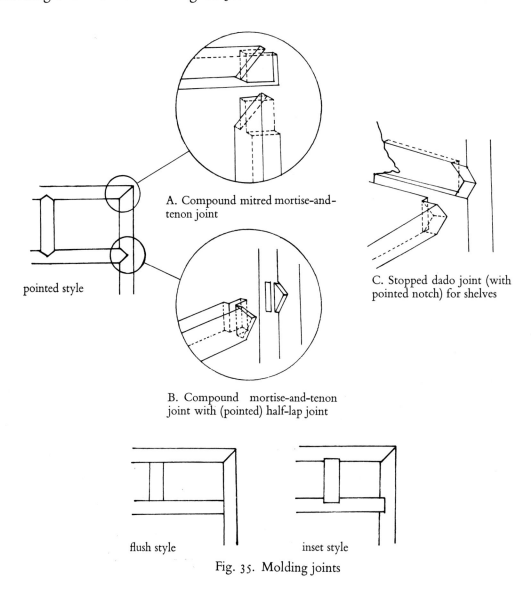

pointed style

A. Compound mitred mortise-and-tenon joint

B. Compound mortise-and-tenon joint with (pointed) half-lap joint

C. Stopped dado joint (with pointed notch) for shelves

flush style   inset style

Fig. 35. Molding joints

Fig. 36. Molding cross-sections

Leg structure. Legged stands (*madae*) are sometimes separated from the frames of large chests—especially in the case of stacked (*nong*) chests—so as to facilitate lifting and moving. The stand serves to elevate the chest, keeping it off the heated (*ondol*) floor. The cabriole style has been most commonly used in leg design—the leg is curved outward at the top and inward further down and ends in a rounded ball or pad, resembling an animal's leg and paw. This basic style, of Chinese inspiration, was also used in European and American furniture design, especially in the first half of the eighteenth century. This kind of elaborately curved design is called *p'unghyŏl* in Korean and is most often seen on furniture for the women's quarters and on "round" serving tables (*soban*) with legs (Plates 88-97).

Most book and display cabinets for the men's quarters have less elaborately carved legs, usually straight (see Plates 122 and 140). Ordinary desks also generally have straight side panels or legs (see Plates 149 and 152). Rectangular serving tables also normally have straight legs or side panels (see Plates 100-106), as did kitchen chests and grain storage boxes (see Plates 84, 86, 87).

Leg structures are usually joined to the body of the chest by tongue and groove and rabbeting or by half-lap and glued (see Figure 37).

Fig. 37. Double-mitred joint for leg of chest stand

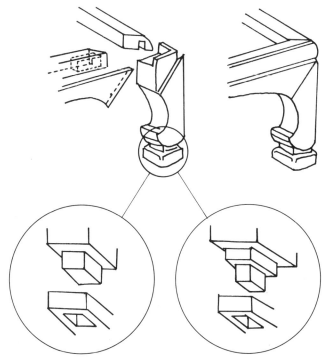

Mortise-and-tenon joints for foot of chest stand leg

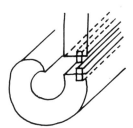

Fig. 38. Full-blind spline joint for scroll foot of chest

Bandaji and coin boxes almost always have two barely noticeable thick boards underneath—extending front to back—to raise them off the heated floor. They were usually attached to the box with glue only. The size of these boards varies according to the size of the piece, although they are seldom more than eight to ten centimeters wide (Plates 28, 35). Occasionally *bandaji* can be found with short, supports that are either attached or are continuations of the side boards (see Plate 29).

Small serving table legs are usually rabbeted and glued to the top structure, and strengthened by wood pegs inserted through the top.

On Buddhist-style study tables, the legs are often elaborately carved with much flourish and detail. The basic leg shape is cabriole, but thinner than the legs of *chang* and *nong*, which, among other things, require more substantial support.

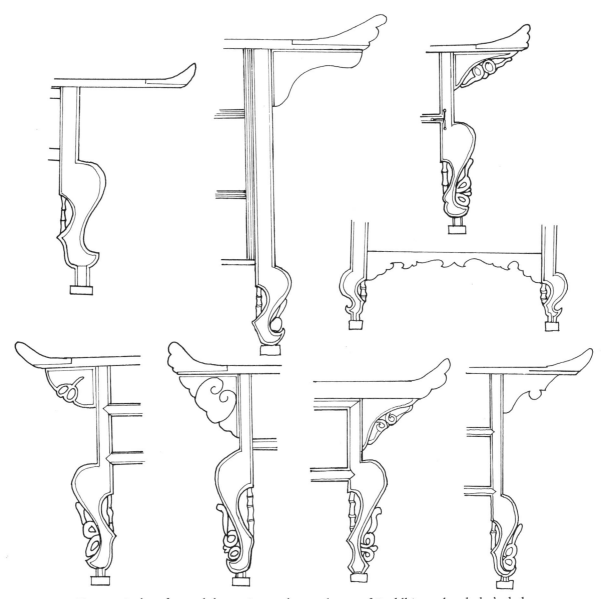

Fig. 39. Styles of carved decoration on legs and tops of Buddhist-style scholar's desks

REGARDING FINISHING processes, Korean sources—both oral and written—tend to differ somewhat in details. The following is an attempt to combine the information gained from various sources into a description of procedures and methods. The material is broken down into fillers and undercoatings, finishes, and final coating.

1. Fillers and undercoatings: Most Korean sources agree on three substances used for this purpose.

a. Clay (*hŭlk*). This material was yellow, red, or occasionally black. It was softened by mixing with water and sometimes vegetable oil and rubbed into the raw wood with a soft cloth. On most furniture, the clay coating was kept thin so as not to obscure the wood grain—it was to protect and darken the wood, not to leave a distinct color, and was rubbed off before becoming completely dry in order to achieve the desired result.

On implements receiving heavy wear *hŭlk* was thickly applied. The finish over this served to retain the clay's color, usually obscuring the grain.

b. Animal blood. Cow's or pig's blood was applied with a cloth to raw wood to protect and darken it. This staining method was used especially in remote rural areas and by the lower classes.

c. Persimmon tannin is an effective protective undercoating, especially for lacquer. This substance is often used in Japan. Persimmon tannin is made from juice of this green fruit; a crude method was to rub wood with green persimmons.

2. Finishes.

a. Perilla oil (*tŭl kirŭm*). Over an undercoating of clay or animal blood, coats of perilla oil were rubbed into the surface with a soft cloth. This was by far the most popular way to finish Yi dynasty furniture. Much furniture is said to have been finished in oil without an undercoating (see Plate 130).

b. Smoking process. A method sometimes used for finishing small objects was to place them over smoke from rice straw that had been aged about one year. This causes the resin in the wood to come to the surface. This resin was then rubbed and spread over the wood with leaves or a cloth.

FINISHES

c. Natural lacquer (*ot-ch'il*). Natural, brown, transparent lacquer from the lacquer tree (*ot-namu*) was applied with a soft cloth over a clay (*hŭlk*) or persimmon tannin undercoating. It was used most often for small objects that saw heavy wear, such as tray-tables (*soban*), large and small mixing bowls, and, sometimes, small boxes for women's incidentals. The best method was to use the sap from the lacquer tree; however, at times workmen used the cruder method of simply rubbing the object with leaves from the lacquer tree. Another crude method was to burn the tree branches and wait for the lacquer (or oil) to come out, and then to apply it to the wood. Usually Yi dynasty lacquered woodwork utilizes natural lacquer, which is sturdy and provides excellent protection for wood. Pigmented lacquer (red or black) was precious and used with restraint on pieces principally for the higher classes of society.

d. Red lacquer (*chu-ch'il*) and black lacquer (*hŭk-ch'il*). Red lacquer is refined lacquer mixed with either iron oxide or cinnabar (mercuric sulfide) pigments, or a mixture of both. Black lacquer normally receives its coloring from iron. Colored lacquer was applied over an undercoating (often persimmon tannin).

In the Orient there are many variations of the lacquering process. Kim Won-Yong, a former director of the National Museum of Korea, has described what must be regarded as an "ideal," though not always practiced, Korean procedure in *Survey of Korean Arts: Fine Arts—I* (Seoul: National Academy, of Arts, 1971), pp. 196–197. Such pieces were intended for royalty, high-ranking government officials, and the aristocracy. A paraphrase of this description is as follows. Pure lacquer is first applied to the wood and dried for seven to ten hours. Then a combination of fifty-five percent (colored) lacquer and forty-five percent rice glue is applied. A piece of thin hemp cloth is applied to the piece, which is then coated with a combination of fifty percent (colored) lacquer, forty-five percent burnt-clay powder, and five percent rice glue by volume. The surface was evened by burnishing with a whetstone. If a mother-of-pearl design was desired, at this stage the shell was stuck on with fish glue, any excess glue being swiftly washed away with boiling water. Around the shell, two (or more?) coatings of a combination of burnt-clay powder (forty percent), colored lacquer (fifty percent), and rice glue (ten percent) were applied, then the object was again burnished with a whetstone until the shell design was exposed to the surface. Another layer—this time thin—of fine colored lacquer was then applied and allowed to dry. The surface was rubbed with the charcoal of the ginkgo tree to expose the shell design again. The finest grade of colored lacquer was then applied, dried, burnished with charcoal, and polished with a smooth cloth containing fine powder and soybean oil (or possibly the oil from nuts).

While this kind of ideal description is helpful to understand the Korean lacquering process, it is hard to imagine that the average Korean craftsman of Yi times was terribly exacting with regard to the above percentages, or that he was careful to apply exactly six layers of lacquer. It is known, too, that Korean lacquer workers often used paper over the wooden object rather than textile. What is important is to know something of the intricacy of the process described above. As suggested in the Preface to this book, more exacting study of traditional Korean lacquering would be a fruitful area for further research. At present, one encounters seemingly contradictory information on the subject; however, such contradiction is natural if a variety of techniques was used, depending on the object and, above all, the craftsman.

e. Decorated ox horn. Ox horn (*hwagak*) was soaked in warm water to soften. It was then flattened, stripped into thin layers, and polished until transparent. These transparent squares or rectangles were painted with landscapes, figures, flowers, and genre scenes, or decorated with gold or silver, and then glued to the wood. This painting was done in reverse, like the Western glass pictures: the painted side was against the wood, visible through the transparent horn. Painted horn is frequently found on women's sewing and incidentals boxes (Plates 17, 66) but is also sometimes seen on larger furniture (Plate 7). The *hwagak* technique is still widely practiced in Korea; however there are few pieces extant that are very old, for horn treated in this way cracks and fades with changes in temperature and moisture.

3. Final coating. Over the dried finish, with a soft cloth the craftsman rubbed on oil of either ginkgo nuts, walnuts, pine nuts, soybeans, castor beans, or sometimes beeswax, among other substances. This served to protect the wood further and to tone down gloss.

Y I FURNITURE FITTINGS were commonly made from yellow brass, white brass, and iron. The white brass alloy includes tin and sometimes nickel in addition to the copper and zinc contained in conventional yellow brass; lead may be included as well. The exact color depends on the proportions of the principal ingredients. Copper is found throughout the Korean peninsula, while tin is mined principally in the Sokcho city area on the east central coast.

As early as the Three Dynasties period (57 B.C.–A.D. 668) metal hinges and pins are known to have been used in upper-class furniture construction. Palanquins for nobility and upper-class officialdom had metal decorations, and chairs and stools were used in officials' offices. Before A.D. 1049, pure copper was normally used for decoration and for strengthening joints on boxes. However, in the later Koryŏ dynasty (938–1392) brass came into more common usage, particularly white brass. Black ironwork on furniture was adopted in the Yi dynasty and was used along with copper and brass.[1]

Shapes of and motifs used in metal fittings on Yi dynasty furniture usually do not exhibit differences according to social class or provenance. However, the following generalizations and observations on the subject are appropriate.

1. Particularly on upper-class furniture, pieces for the men's and women's quarters frequently display differences in metalwork. Women's furniture tends to be more highly decorated and sometimes has brasswork with incised designs, usually happiness and longevity motifs.

2. Generally speaking, red and black lacquered trim on headside (*mŏrijang*) and multileveled chests (*chang*) was reserved for use by the members of the extended royal family, who were mostly resident around Seoul and on Kanghwa Island (Plates 5, 13).

3. The phoenix on incised metalwork was generally employed only on furniture for the extended royal family. Other classes used the bat, particularly for handles and

METAL FITTINGS

sometimes for frontal brass. The bat form appears as handles on royal furniture as well.

4. Until the last years of the dynasty, the regions of Korea from Kyŏnggi and Kangwŏn provinces south favored furniture that was fairly subdued in ornamentation. In most cases, metalwork appears mainly to complement wood grains, which provide the basic decorative focus (Plate 40, Kyŏnggi; Plate 151, Ch'ungch'ŏng; Plate 85, Kyŏngsang).

5. Traditional furniture from the northern areas is more likely to have abundant metalwork on the front than that from the south. Woods plentiful in the north were without decorative grains, therefore there is more emphasis on decorative metalwork than on wood grain. The *ssung-ssung-i* style of *bandaji* displays an abundance of finely wrought openwork iron (Plate 31), while the Pyŏngyang style often has a large amount of brass extensively incised with happiness and longevity motifs (Plate 32).

6. In the late years of the dynasty and the years immediately after, there was an increase in the use of metalwork and decorative embellishment on much upper-class women's furniture. So the more brass that is used, the more likely it is that a piece is from the early years of the twentieth century rather than from earlier times (see Plate 6).

7. Most kitchen cabinets and grain storage boxes have the same simple and subdued iron fittings, regardless of provenance.

8. The style and arrangement of ironwork on Cheju Island *bandaji* is characteristic only of Cheju pieces. Hinges have a modified swallowtail design with rounded ends; the front bottom of the *bandaji* often has a chrysanthemum-shaped metal ornament with a Buddhist swastika at the center (see Plate 33). The rounded swallowtail hinge motif is found, too, on small *bandaji* from the coastal area and islands in the southwestern part of the peninsula (see Plate 36).

9. The ironwork on upper-class *bandaji* from the Chŏlla region is generally similar and shows little variation in style, particularly the hinges and plate for the lock (see Plates 1, 2).

10. The *bandaji* identified with Kanghwa Island near Seoul usually had a bottle-gourd-shaped hinge on the center of the front and round ornaments on each side of the lock.

11. Chests from the Kyŏnggi, Kangwŏn, North Kyŏngsang, and North Ch'ungch'ŏng areas often display a similarity of styles, woods, and decorative metalwork, making accurate identification of provenance difficult.

12. Yi furniture makers were itinerate to some extent. They were sometimes hired by upper-class families outside their native regions to construct furniture for a new household or to make new furniture for an old household. In such cases, they would usually retain the styling and flavor of the furniture of their native areas. Thus, pieces with decorative characteristics, including metalwork, of one region may be found in alien places. Sometimes, too, furniture makers for the middle and lower classes peddled their wares at various marketplaces over a wide area.

DECORATION AND SYMBOLISM

It is necessary to discuss the symbolic motifs utilized in metal fittings, inlay, and carving on Yi dynasty furniture. In Korea, many of the symbolic decorations found in the traditional arts and crafts have widely recognized meanings. At this point in time, however, some seem to be merely decorative, and the meanings are at best matters of conjecture. The motifs discussed below are largely Chinese in origin, but in many instances any original significance has been modified or even lost over the centuries. With these points in mind, it is the intent in this chapter not to engage in hypothetical discussion concerning ancient origins of particular symbols, but rather to attempt to indicate what they meant, if anything, to the people of Yi dynasty times who were exposed to them.

Among the most widely understood symbols in traditional Korea have been those for happiness (*pok* or *haeng-bok*) and long life (*chang-su*). An academic distinction is sometimes made between happiness meaning good fortune (福) and happiness meaning joy or felicity (喜); in popular usage, however, this distinction in unclear, and the two seem to go hand in hand. The actual Chinese character for happiness-joy is frequently seen in art in general, including furniture decoration; for

ten longevity motifs

plum blossoms

Fig. 40. Auspicious motifs

example, the famous "double happiness" motif—a combination of two felicity characters—is often seen on women's chests (see Plate 46). In the relatively rigid Confucian social structure of Korea's mid-Yi dynasty—the seventeenth and eighteenth centuries—the phoenix was reserved as a special happiness motif for royalty, while the bat was used by the *yangbang* aristocracy and merchant class. Such distinctions, however, tended to break down in the dynasty's later years. It is somewhat puzzling that the bat would be selected as a happiness symbol. One explanation offered by scholars—though not generally perceived by the average layman—is that in former times the Chinese characters for happiness connoting good fortune and for bat were pronounced the same in both Chinese (*fu*) and Korean (*pok*). In Korea at least, any homophonic relationship that might have existed has been lost, and the bat is simply accepted as a symbol of happiness for whatever reasons, not the least of which may be that the bat shape is quite adaptable for decorative stylization.

There are numerous symbols for longevity; however, the most widely recognized are those the Koreans call the "ten long-life symbols" (*sip-jang saeng*). Depending on the source, the ten cited vary somewhat, resulting in a country-wide total of fifteen or so; those most frequently mentioned include the tortoise, crane, pine tree, deer, rock, cloud, bamboo, water, sun, and a kind of mythical fungus called *pulloch'o* in Korean and *ling zhi* in Chinese. In Chinese lore, the *pulloch'o* is said to be divine, bringing immortality. The tortoise, crane, and deer are known for their longevity, while rocks, clouds, water, and the sun certainly belong to the ages. Bamboo is hard and durable, persistent in its growth patterns. The pine is an evergreen and, like bamboo, relatively resistant to the elements. A popular subject of traditional Chinese and Korean painting and embroidery is the ten long-life symbols portrayed together. As such they are blended into a scene reflecting tranquillity and bliss, a kind of paradise. Many of these long-life symbols are inscribed on the brasswork of the *bandaji* in Plate 32.

Other decorative symbols on furniture that are sometimes identified with long life

Fig. 41. Auspicious motifs

landscape

crane and clouds

landscape

bamboo

are the butterfly and the "heavenly peach." The latter is often used as a handle (Plate 59).

The stylization of the south gate of a city wall is a motif that seems strange to Westerners at first. The south gate was usually the principal one, thus finding its way into the vocabulary of auspicious decorative motifs.

There are generally recognized traditional symbols and motifs used on furniture besides those representing happiness and long life. The traditional Taoist design seen in much Korean metalwork, known in Korea as *t'aeguk*, is derived from the Chinese yin-yang. The *t'aeguk* design, based upon the interlocking yin-yang symbol, designates motion—Taoism maintains that nothing is ever repeated exactly and that only the concept of change itself is unchangeable. From the Taoist perspective, the circle is symbolic of heaven and the square, earth; heaven and earth are dichotomized but seen as two-in-one. It has been suggested by Korean scholars that a circular shape found imposed upon a square shape represents heaven-in-earth. Usually this design found in Korean metalwork can be assumed to reflect these Taoist precepts. Probably the best-known contemporary example of the Taoist-inspired design is on the Korean national flag.

Taoist philosophy also offers trigrams, which connote cyclical patterns relating to different kinds of change. Usually appearing in circular arrangement, the eight trigrams are composed of solid and broken lines, illustrating the change patterns. The solid lines are associated with yang, the broken ones with yin. These eight trigrams have the following accepted designations:

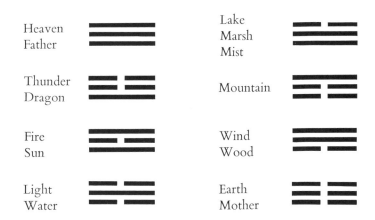

geese

Fig. 42. Auspicious motifs

The Buddhist swastika can be found carved into various pieces of furniture, particularly Buddhist study tables and book cabinets. It is frequently seen also in the metalwork of clothing chests. The origins of the swastika are said to predate the advent of Buddhism, though in China, Korea, and Japan it accompanies Buddhism. It has many meanings, among them perfection, harmony, and happiness.

Of flower designs, four are commonly accepted symbols of the seasons: peony (spring); lotus (summer); chrysanthemum (autumn), and plum blossom (winter). The lotus is also associated with Buddhism. The term *sup'allyŏn* refers to a commonly used shape for the central metal piece on much Korean furniture; literally, "water plant," the *sup'allyŏn* is considered to be based on the lotus shape. Another flower, the pear blossom, is said by some to be a sign of longevity because the tree itself is long lived. It is tenuous to suggest specific meanings for most flower designs; it is better to simply accept them as decorative embellishment. The same might be said for the swallowtail, which is a popular and appropriate shape for decorative hinges on the front of various styles of chests. The fish in general is symbolic of abundance and prosperity; the fish-shaped lock is ubiquitous on the peninsula.

Frets and scrolls are often found on the legs and bases of large chests (Plate 14). Some scholars of traditional symbolism see archaic pictographs representing clouds and thunder in various geometric designs and fret patterns; with Korean furniture, however, it is probably better to see these simply as decorative carvings. The bottle gourd is widely considered to be a receptacle for medicine. This is because a gourd is held in the hand of Li Dieguai, one of the eight immortals of Taoism. They are well known in Korea, among other reasons, because of the Sŏkkuram grotto near Kyŏngju, which houses stone carvings of a large Buddha image surrounded by these immortals—this group of eighth century carvings is considered by many to be among the great art works of Asia and the world. Its two most famous figures are those of the Buddha and the immortal holding the gourd.

The dragon should be mentioned—unlike the fearful Western monster, the Eastern mythological creature is reflective of strength and goodness. Either coiled or straight,

double-happiness characters   longevity character   Taoist trigrams

Buddhist swastika   Taoist *t'aeguk* motif variant   Taoist *t'aeguk* motif   Taoist *t'aeguk* motif variant

Fig. 43. Auspicious motifs

it provides a useful shape in artistic design. One more motif with a generally accepted meaning is that of a pair of mandarin ducks, which are seen in traditional Korean wedding ceremonies and symbolize marital fidelity and bliss.

The tiger is considered an animal of courage and is a symbol of protection against evil spirits. The dragon and tiger are often portrayed together and are seen as double protection for a household.

Other decorative shapes can be identified, but again attempts to read definite symbolic meanings into most of them is a tenuous enterprise at best. In conclusion, it is important to understand that much that might appear to be merely decorative embellishment on Korean furniture actually has symbolic content, usually associated with happiness and long life. It is probably equally important not to grope for symbolic meanings when such are not clearly there, at least in the popular mind.

1. Chinese historical records of the third century A.D. indicate that iron was then being produced in Pyŏnhan in southern Korea. See Sohn Pow-key, Kim Chol-choon and Hong Yi-sup, *The History of Korea* (Seoul: Korean National Commission for UNESCO, 1970), p. 31; and Sohn Pow-key, *Early Korean Typography* (Seoul: The Korean Library Research Institute, 1971), pp. 31–41. Parts of the above material also were derived from an interview with Professor Sohn Pow-key.

Hinges (kyŏng-ch'ŏp). There were two main types of door hinges in Yi dynasty furniture construction. One, the pin-and-eye pivot, whose variations are illustrated in Figure 44, was functional and not decorative. Traditionally, these were made of wrought iron; however, in the late dynasty brass was often used. This pin-and-eye pivot type of hinge was not common; it is found mainly on many-leveled book chests and on kitchen cabinets.

The most widely used type of hinge is essentially the same as the hinge most familiar to the West. It lies flat on the chest, one wing being attached to the chest body and the other to the door, lid, or opening panel. Its structure allows free play for decorative embellishment. The vast variety of shapes are illustrated in the drawings that follow.

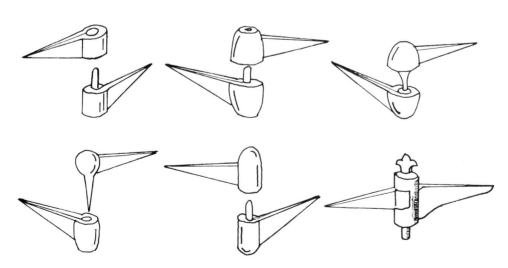

Fig. 44. Pin-and-eye pivot hinges

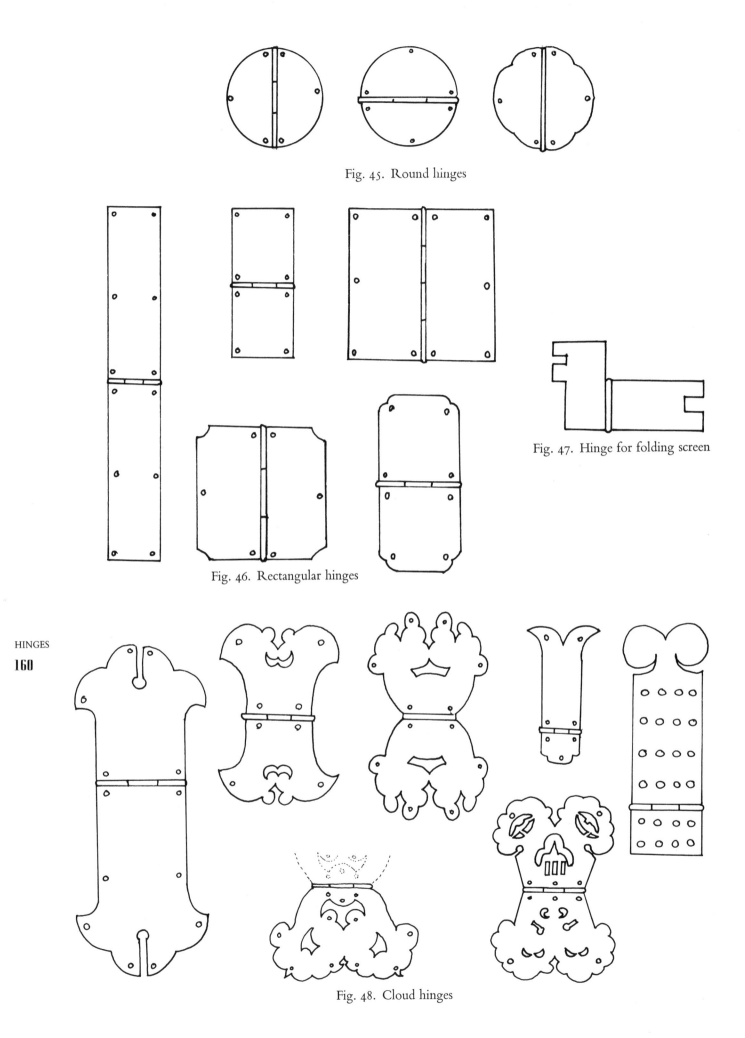

Fig. 45. Round hinges

Fig. 47. Hinge for folding screen

Fig. 46. Rectangular hinges

Fig. 48. Cloud hinges

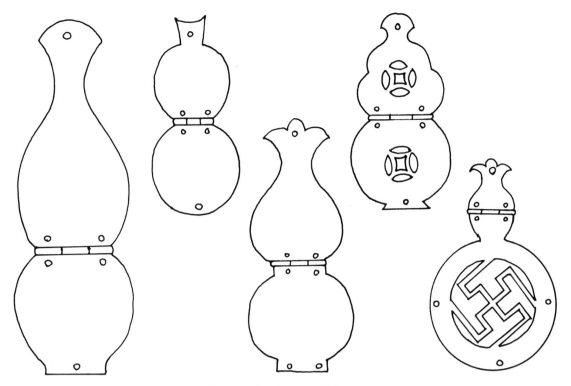

Fig. 49. Bottle-gourd hinges

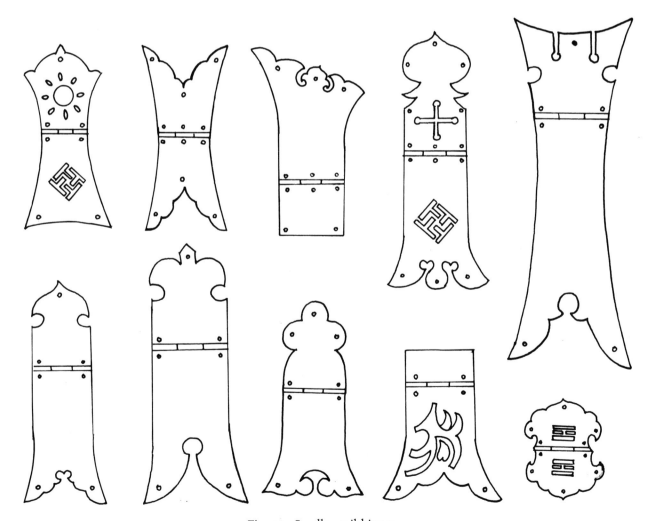

Fig. 50. Swallowtail hinges

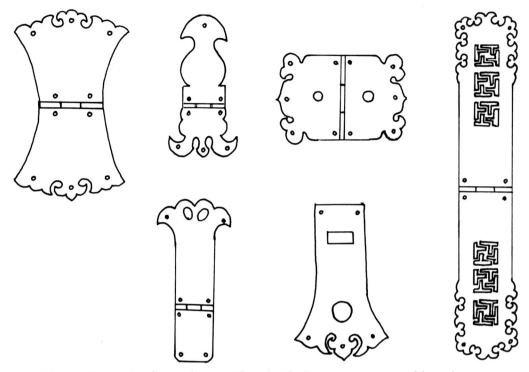

Fig. 51. Longevity fungus hinges. This motif often appears as a trifoliate form decorating the edges of metal fittings.

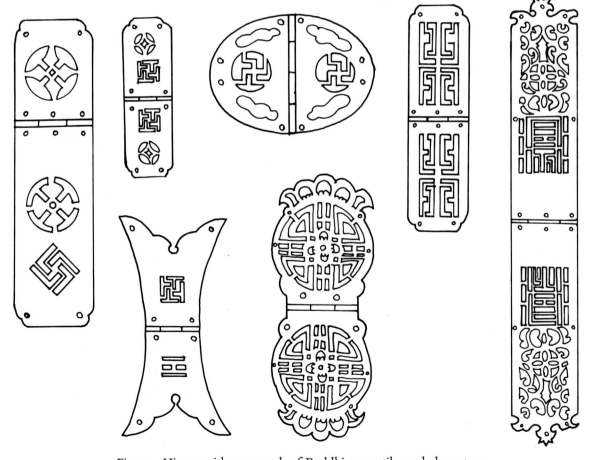

Fig. 52. Hinges with openwork of Buddhist swastika and characters

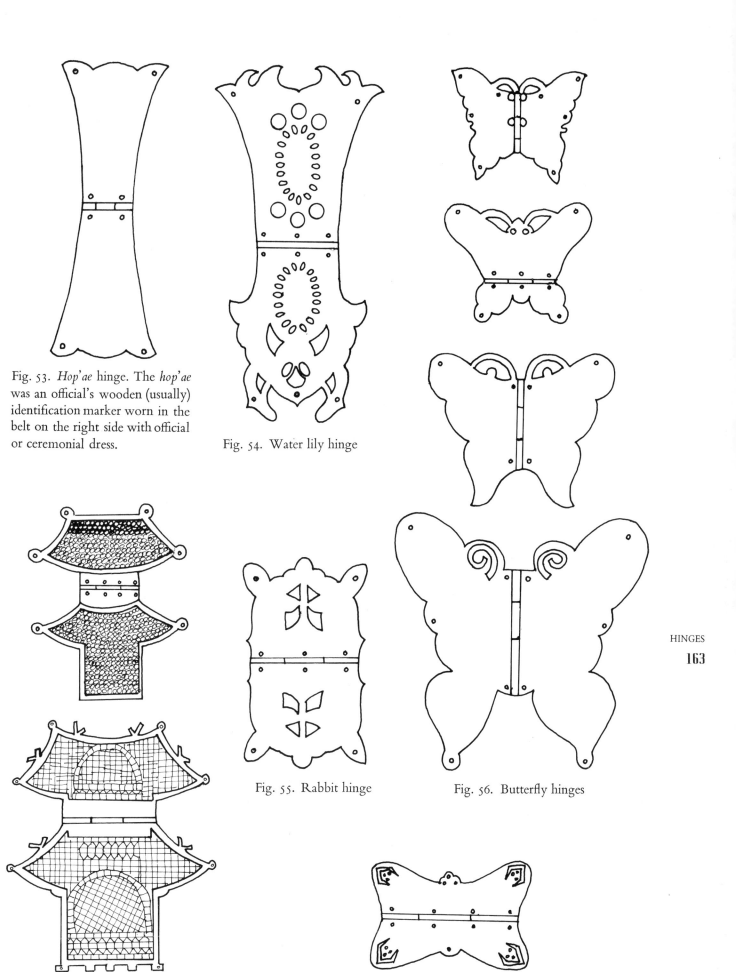

Fig. 53. *Hop'ae* hinge. The *hop'ae* was an official's wooden (usually) identification marker worn in the belt on the right side with official or ceremonial dress.

Fig. 54. Water lily hinge

Fig. 55. Rabbit hinge

Fig. 56. Butterfly hinges

Fig. 57. South Gate (of city wall) hinges

Fig. 58. Bat hinge

Handles (tŭlsoi). Like hinges, furniture handles are often in traditional symbolic shapes. Some are attached with single hooks and others with double hooks. Single-hook handles are usually found on men's stationery cabinets (including the *mungap* style, with doors lifting up and out), writing tables, and small drawers on large tiered chests. Figure 59 illustrates various designs of one-hook handles, and Figure 60 those of two-hook handles.

Some of the more literal and obvious designs include the bat (15); pear blossom (8); butterfly (13); key (2); and perhaps pomegranate (11). Number 7 is a balsam blossom (*pong-sung sŏn-hwa*). Number 6 is the interlocking design (here of squares but usually of circles) known as the "seven treasures" (*ch'ilbo*). Number 1 is sometimes seen as the "heavenly peach," upside down.

There are no particular regional variations to be found in handle design—all styles can be seen on chests from throughout the peninsula.

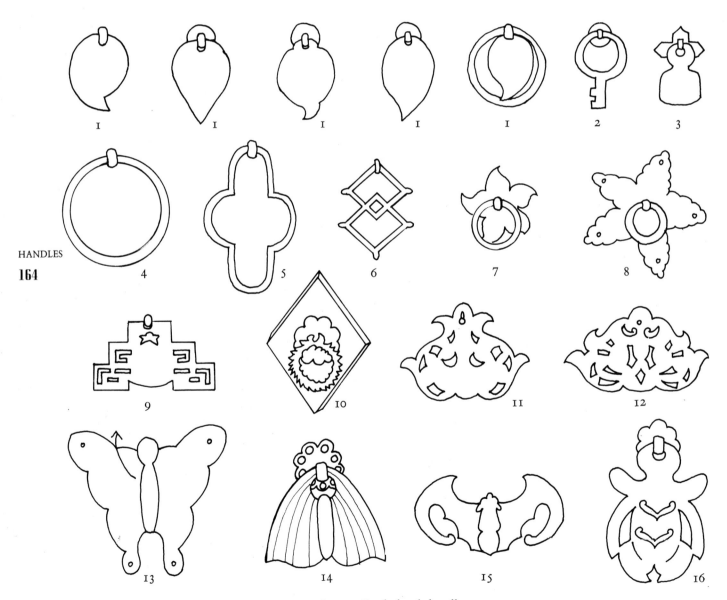

HANDLES
164

Fig. 59. Single-hook handles

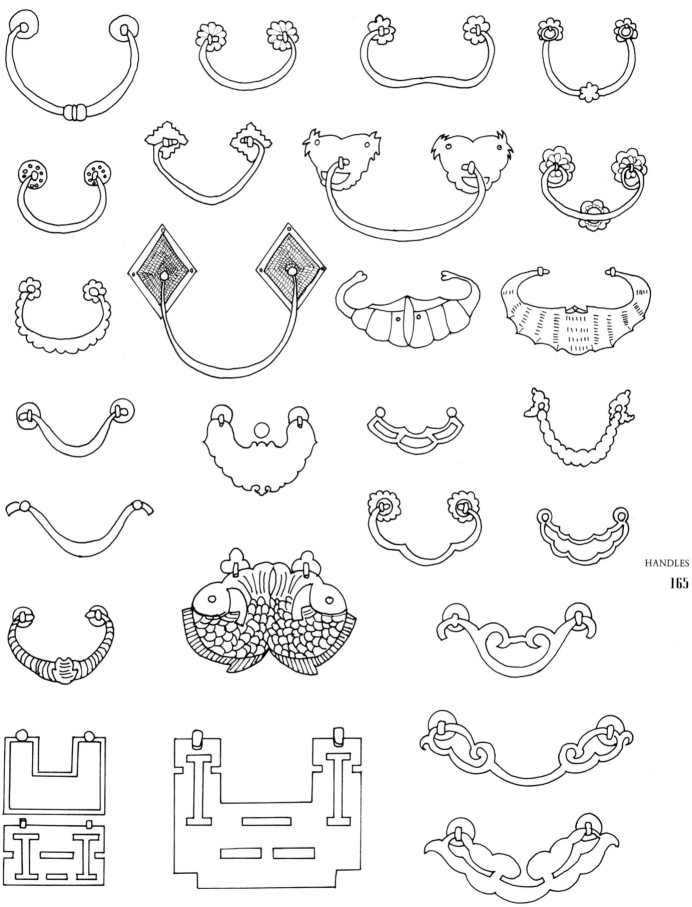

Fig. 60. Double-hook handles

Fig. 61. Double-hook handles with bat and butterfly back plates

Locks. In Yi dynasty metalwork, locks were decorative as well as functional. There is evidence that clasp locks were used as early as the Three Kingdoms period (57 B.C.–A.D. 668), however other styles apparently were not used until the Yi dynasty (1392–1911).

Various styles of locks and keys are illustrated in Figures 62–67. The vertical lock was sometimes used on upper-class tiered and stacked chests, though this type is not common. The more elaborate the shape and decorative incising, the more probable it is that a lock was used by the upper classes. A detachable lock with intricate incising is seldom found with the chest to which it originally belonged; such locks themselves have become collectors' items.

Fig. 62. Vertical locks, used on chests with double doors

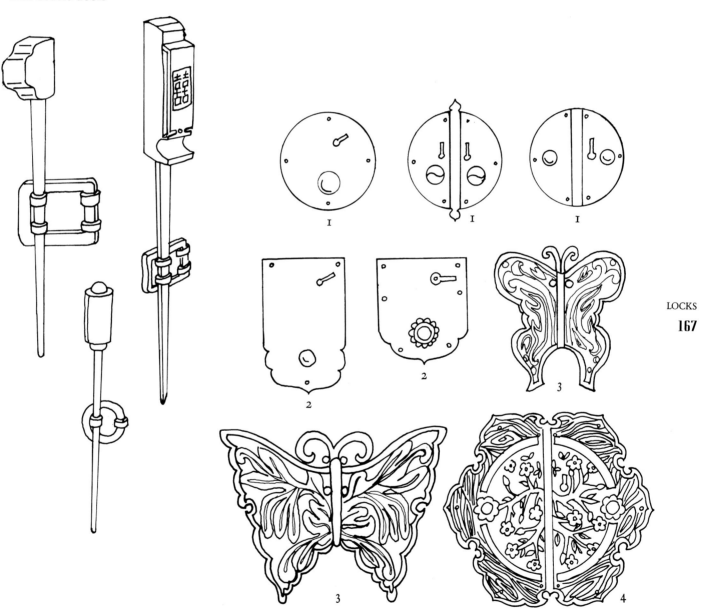

Fig. 63. Keyhole lock plates, with shapes of moon (1), *mangdu* plant (2), butterfly (3), and longevity fungus (each lobe of hexagon of 4). Keyholes of (3) are hidden.

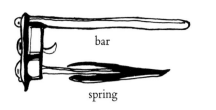

bar

spring

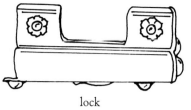

lock

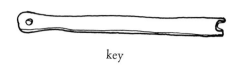

key

Fig. 64. Clasp lock structure

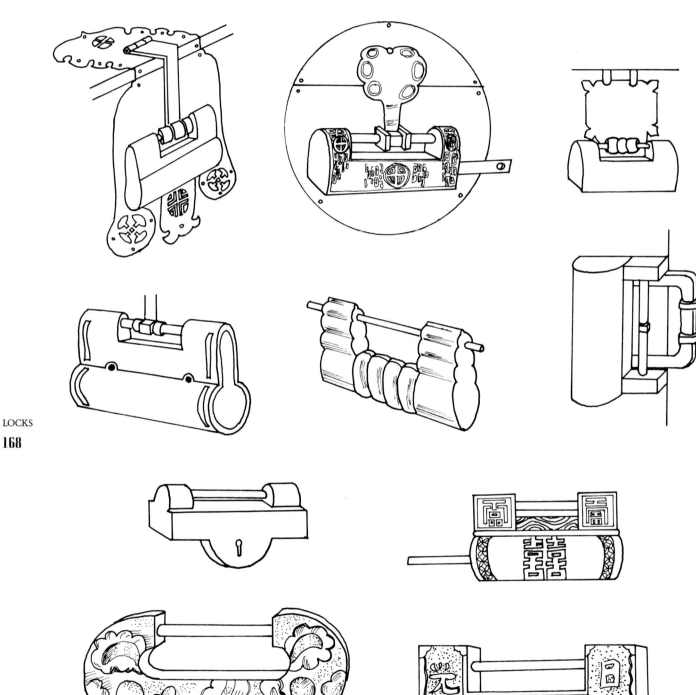

Fig. 65. Clasp locks

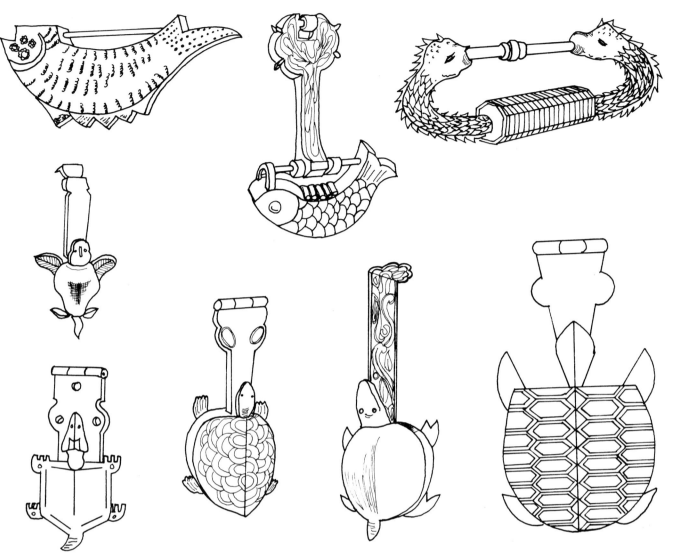

Fig. 66. Tongue fasteners and turtle, fish, and dragon locks

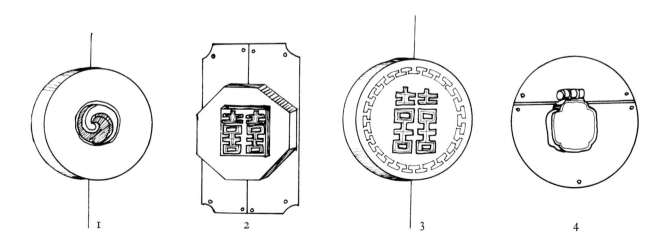

Fig. 67. Case locks with designs of Taoist *t'aeguk* symbol (1) and double-happiness characters (2) and (3); (4) is a stylized turtle shape.

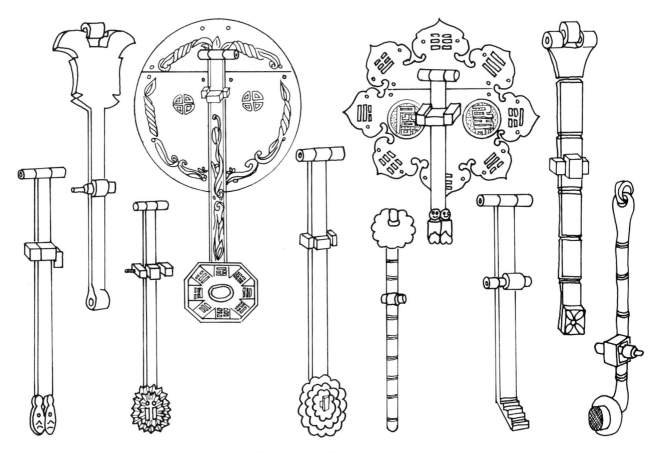

Fig. 68. Long tongue fasteners, used on top-opening boxes and chests

Fig. 69. Tongue fasteners for use on *bandaji* chests. The fastener is attached to the *bandaji*, and the bar of the clasp lock fits into it.

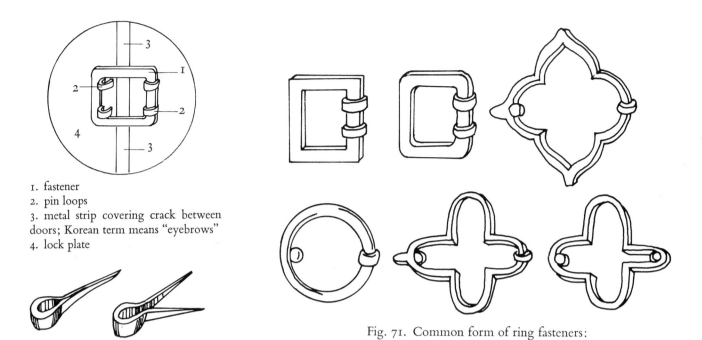

1. fastener
2. pin loops
3. metal strip covering crack between doors; Korean term means "eyebrows"
4. lock plate

pin loops

Fig. 70. Structure of ring fasteners used on outward-opening double doors.

Fig. 71. Common form of ring fasteners: round, square, and foliate

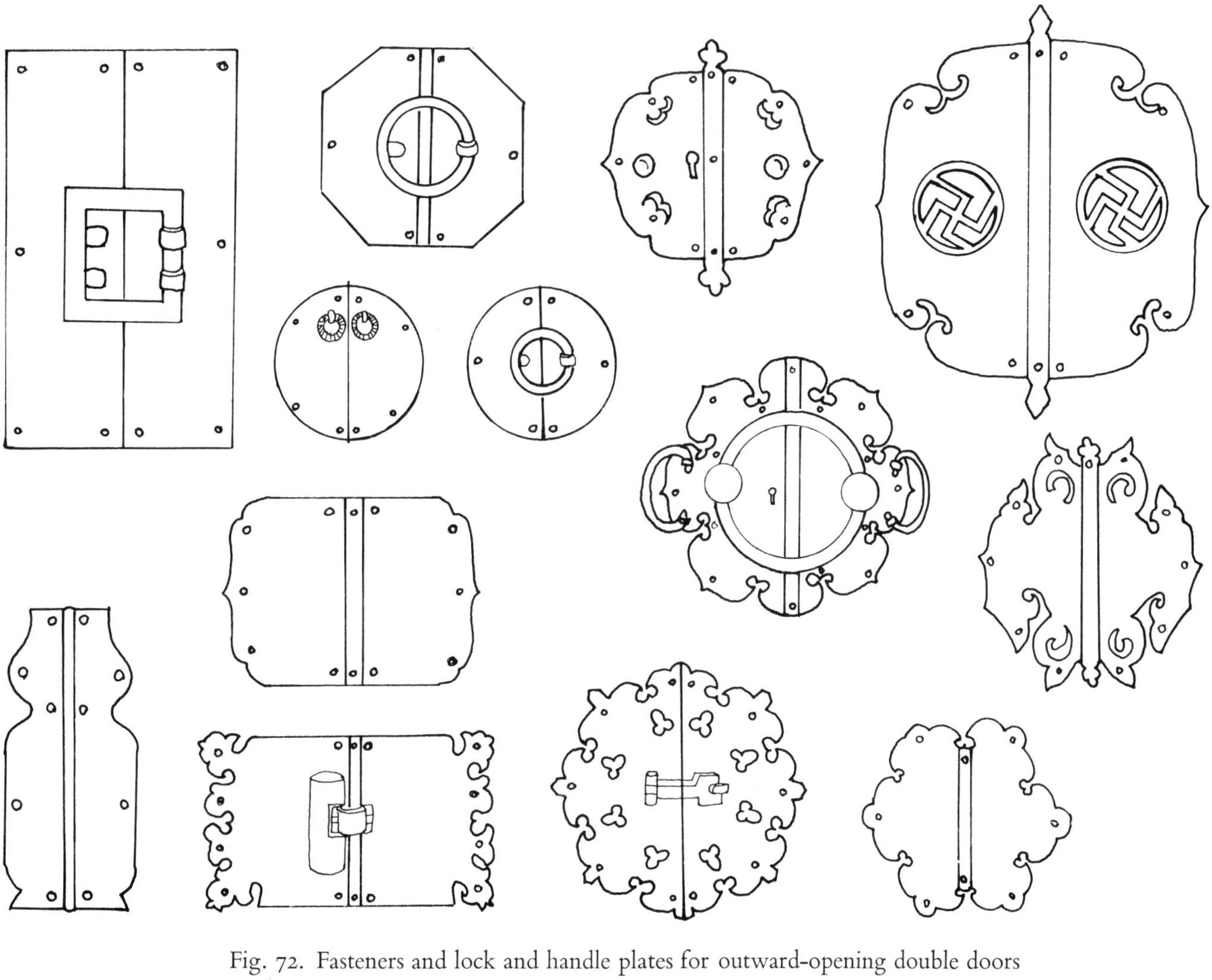

Fig. 72. Fasteners and lock and handle plates for outward-opening double doors

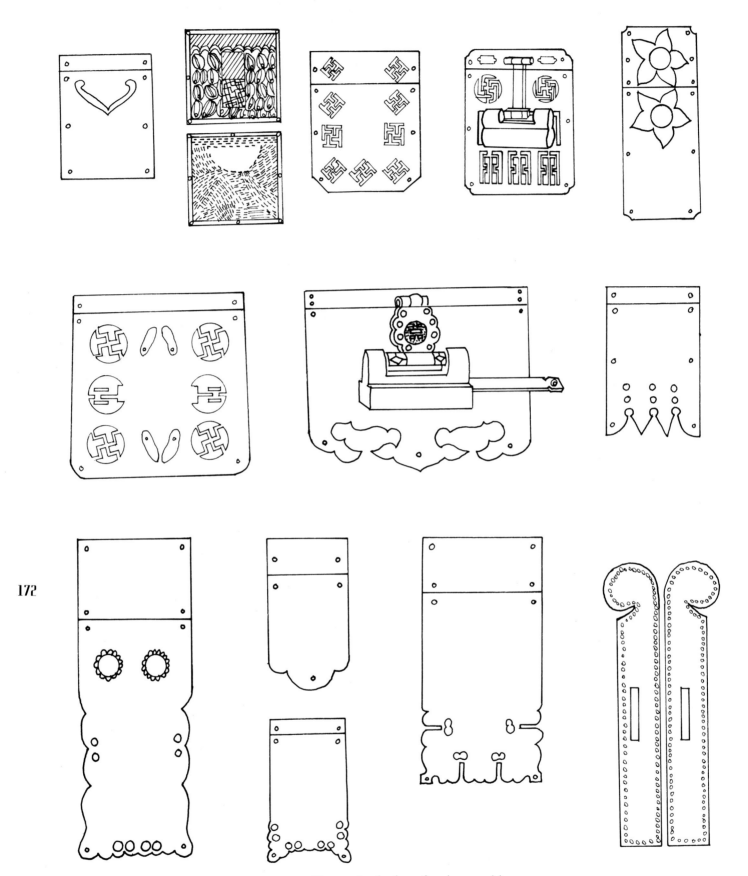

Fig. 73. Lock plates for chests and boxes
(*bandaji*, coin chests, etc.)

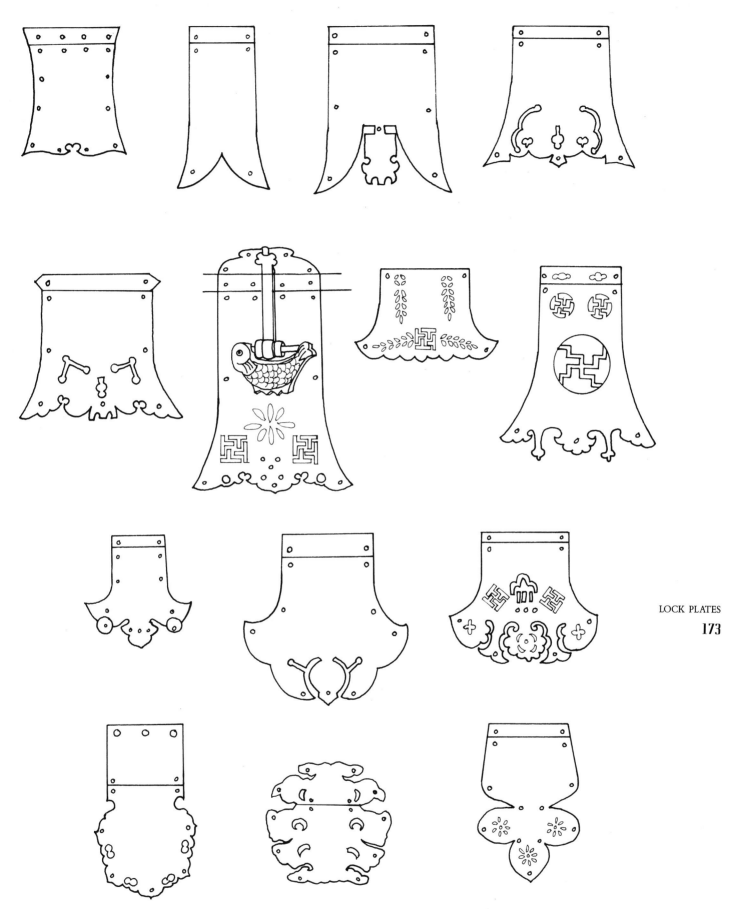

Fig. 74. Lock plates for chests and boxes
(*bandaji*, coin chests, etc.)

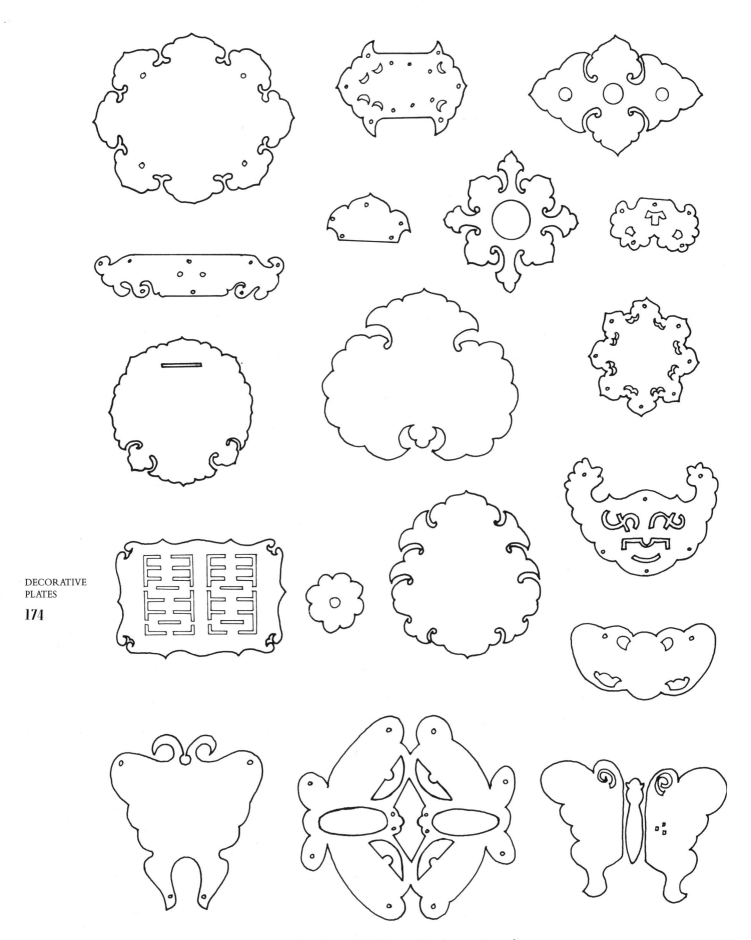

Fig. 75. Decorative plates and fittings found on various chest types

Staples and corner pieces (kamjabi). Some metalwork on corners serves to protect and strengthen the joints or wood, while some seems merely decorative, though clearly derived from functional pieces.

Fig. 76. Basic corner braces, found on all types of chests and boxes throughout Korea.

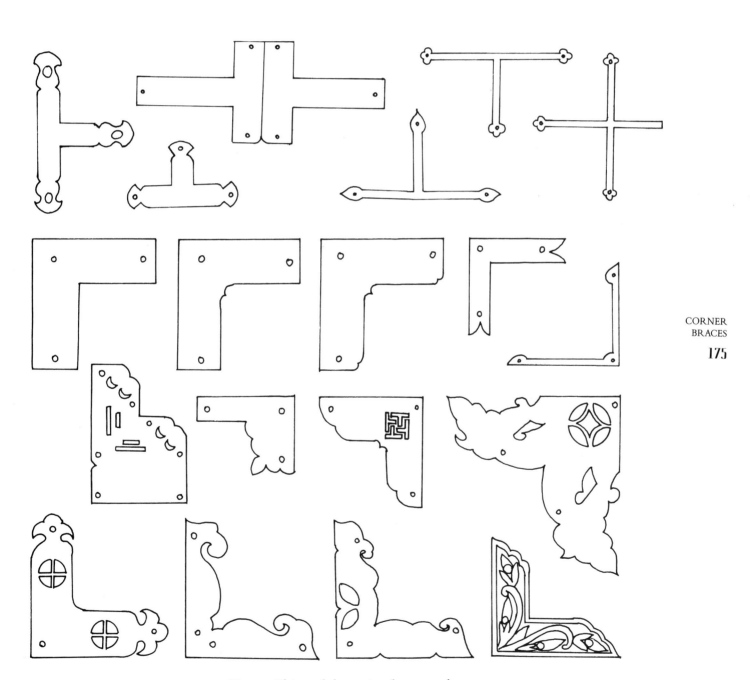

Fig. 77. Plain and decorative flat corner braces

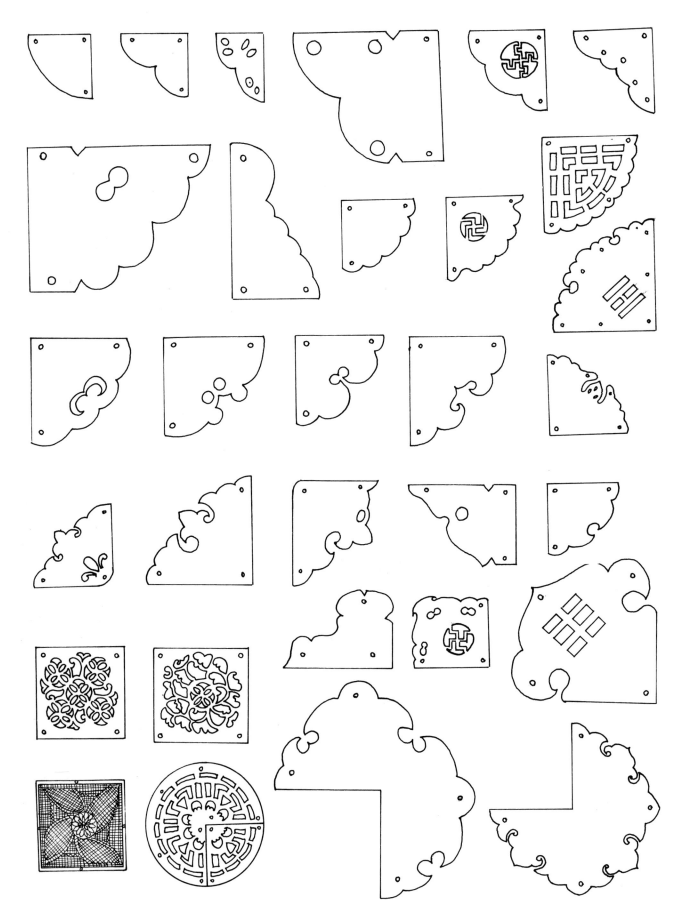

176

Fig. 78. Decorative flat corner braces

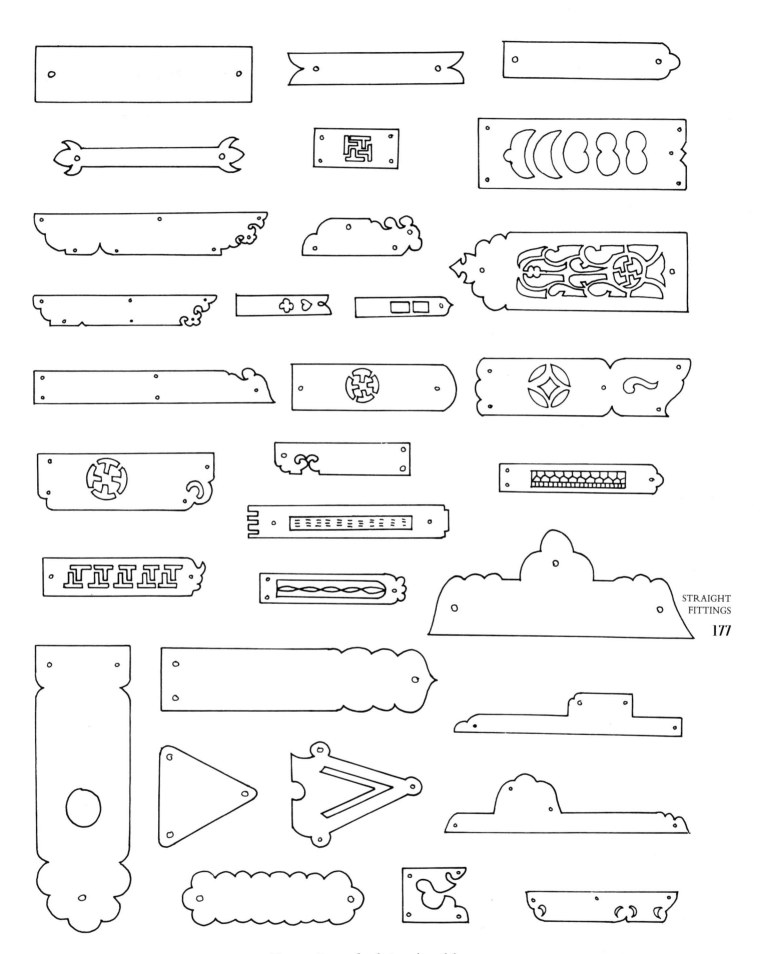

Fig. 79. Long, flat fittings (mostly)

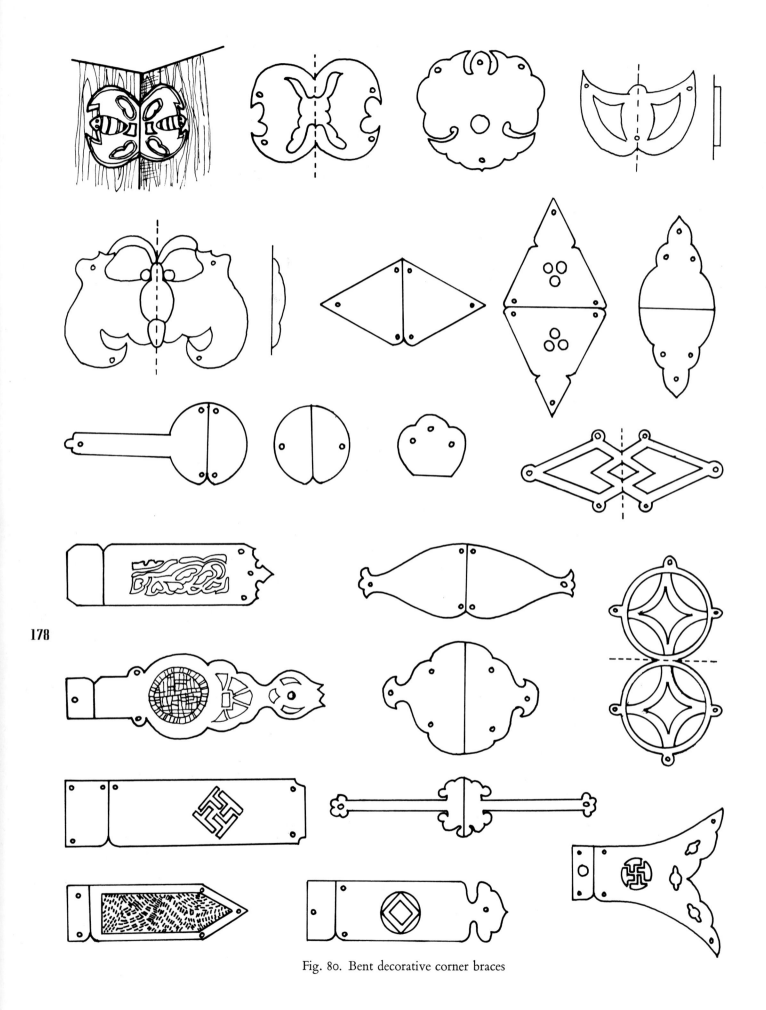

178

Fig. 80. Bent decorative corner braces

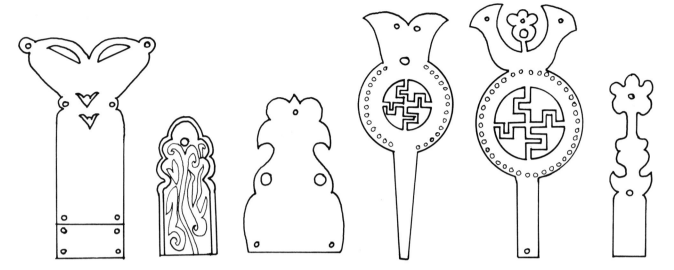

Fig. 81. Bent decorative corner braces

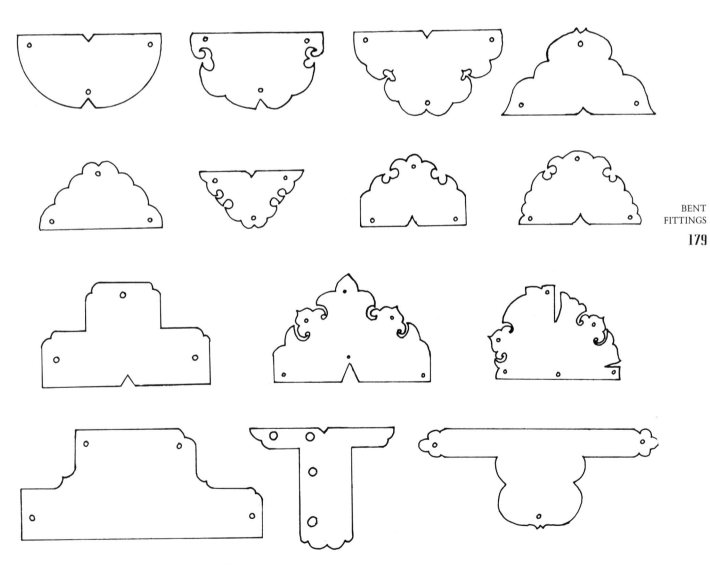

Fig. 82. Bent fittings for chest legs and stands

Nail covers (kwangdujŏng). These were used to conceal ordinary pegs or dowels used in furniture construction as well as for ornamentation alone. Relatively small in size, they are also found on front gate panels of traditional houses.

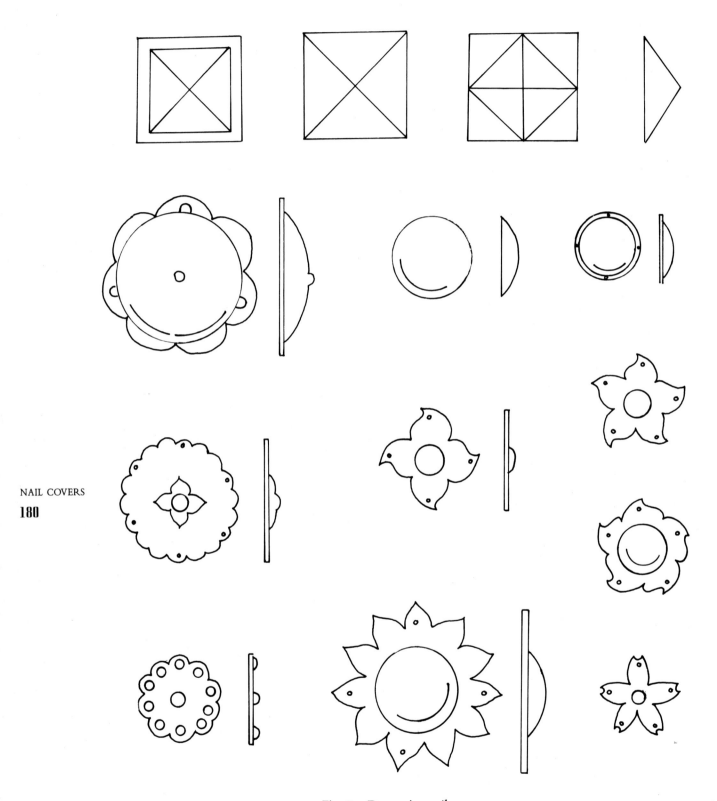

Fig. 83. Decorative nail covers

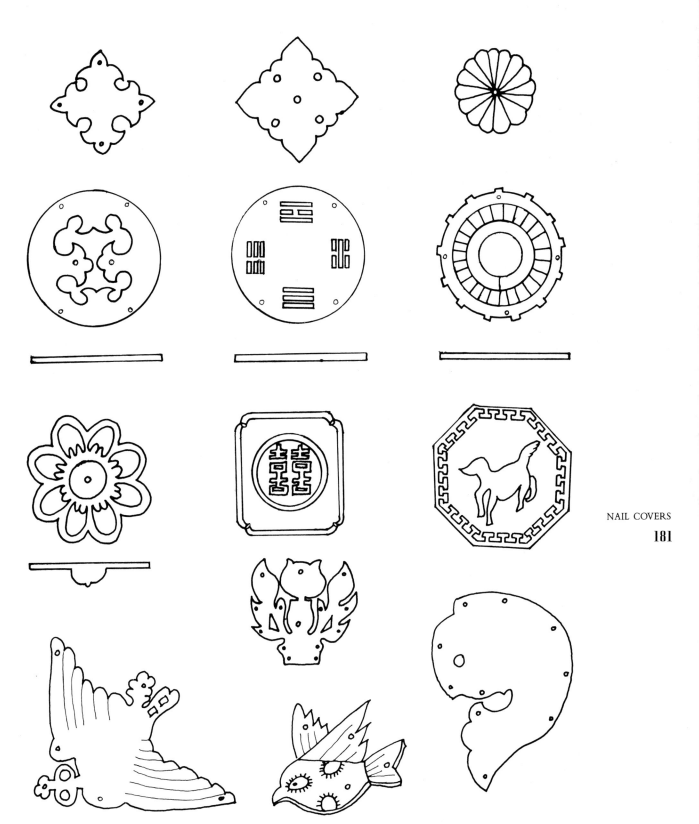

Fig. 84. Decorative nail covers

THE YI DYNASTY cabinetmaker produced furniture on commission for or by arrangement with a particular household or else he made relatively simple pieces to be sold in the marketplace. Either way, his tools were his livelihood. Even though little systematic study has been made of Yi dynasty woodworking tools and thus little general information is available on this subject, some indication of the Korean woodworker's tools in this book is important and adds to both the specialist student's and casual collector's appreciation of traditional furniture.

Tool design is, of course, intimately tied to the blacksmith's trade and to the needs of each craft. The cabinetmaker's tools were generally the same throughout the Korean peninsula, with some local and individual variations. Such tools were probably made by local blacksmiths, but tool handles, as is common in the Orient, were made by the craftsmen themselves to fit their own hands and custom.

Thus, a Yi dynasty woodcraftsman's tools have their own flavor, but most are recognizable to the Westerner. Koreans often refer to themselves as having an acute sense of touch; such would be especially true of the craftsman, who worked so closely with his materials.

Perhaps the most well-known Korean woodworker's and carpenter's tool is the ink-line holder (*mokt'ong*), which is said to have been the Yi craftsman's favorite tool. This object serves the same function as the Western chalk line, but in Korea the string was blackened by passing it through cotton kept wet with black ink, and a straight black line was left on the wood when the taut, ink-damp string was snapped against the wood surface. The *mokt'ong* has a well to hold the ink-dampened cotton and a reel for the string. An apprentice spent several years learning the woodworking craft, and his ability to use and then to make an ink-line holder was an important indication of his expertise. To construct one well was an important mark of status in the profession.

The *mokt'ong* today has become a collector's item, so much more attention has been paid to this object than to the adzes, saws, files, and chisels of the woodworker.

183

TOOLS

In essence, a *mokt'ong* is a work of sculpture. The most common shape is a stylized turtle, though pieces are found in animal, bird, and fruit shapes. Some of these ink-line holders are elaborate, while some are quite primitive or are stylized almost to the point of becoming minimalist art.

A hardwood without knots or weaknesses was the ideal material for a *mokt'ong*; such wood allowed the carving to be free of blemishes and insured that the piece would last. The more primitive *mokt'ong*, however, seem to have been made by craftsmen who gleefully ignored such niceties.

A master woodworker usually owned several ink-line holders. When he handed down one of his own to an apprentice, it was considered a great honor. In a sense, the *mokt'ong* epitomizes the Korean woodworking tradition; it was a test for the young craftsman to use one and, later, to make one properly. Other tools, of course, were equally important for the functions served, but they were not as symbolic as the *mokt'ong*.

The sketches that follow represent a variety of woodworker's tools, including the *mokt'ong*. These are but a sampling of such tools; a comprehensive collection of Yi dynasty furniture-maker's tools apparently still needs to be compiled and documented.

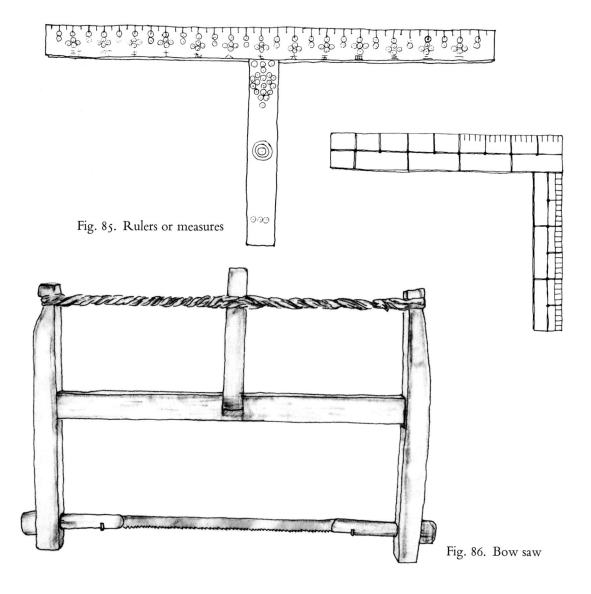

Fig. 85. Rulers or measures

Fig. 86. Bow saw

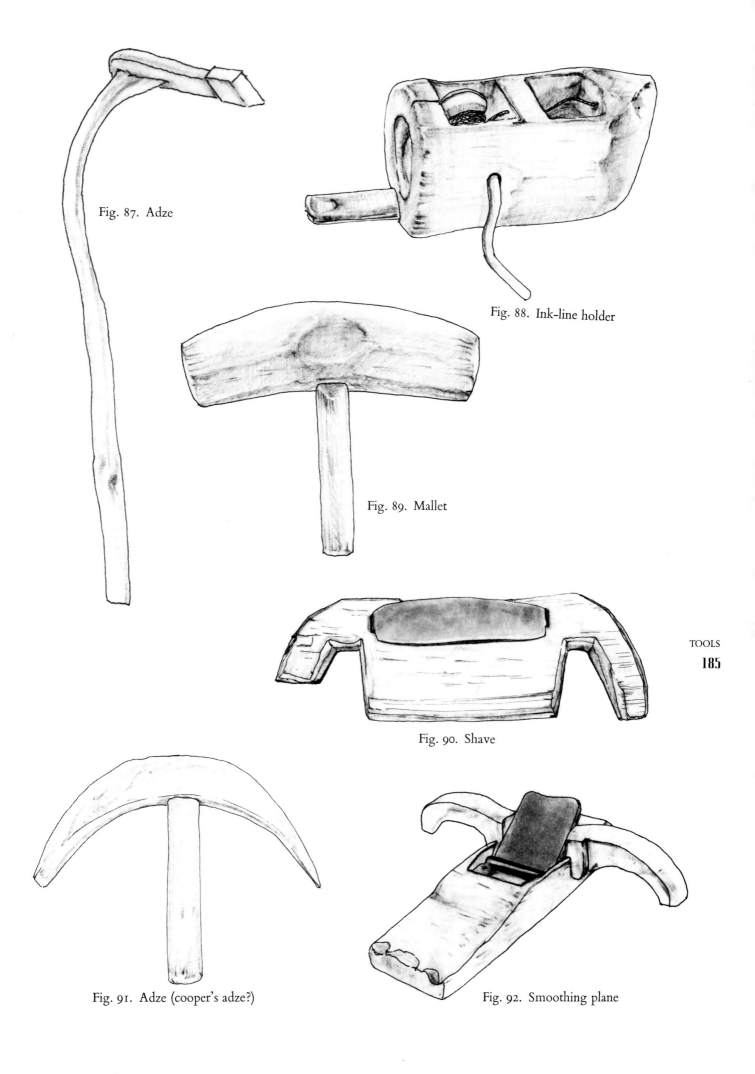

Fig. 87. Adze

Fig. 88. Ink-line holder

Fig. 89. Mallet

Fig. 90. Shave

Fig. 91. Adze (cooper's adze?)

Fig. 92. Smoothing plane

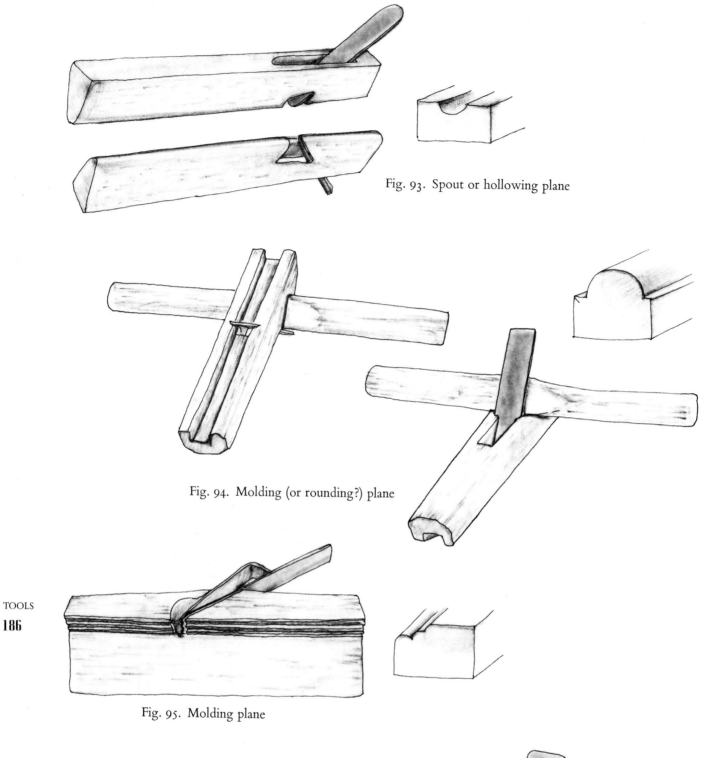

Fig. 93. Spout or hollowing plane

Fig. 94. Molding (or rounding?) plane

Fig. 95. Molding plane

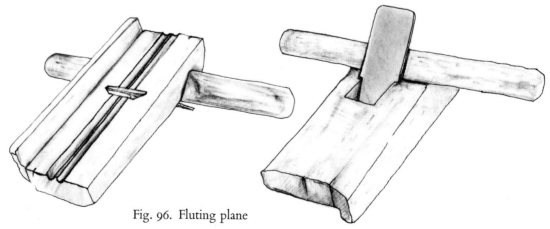

Fig. 96. Fluting plane

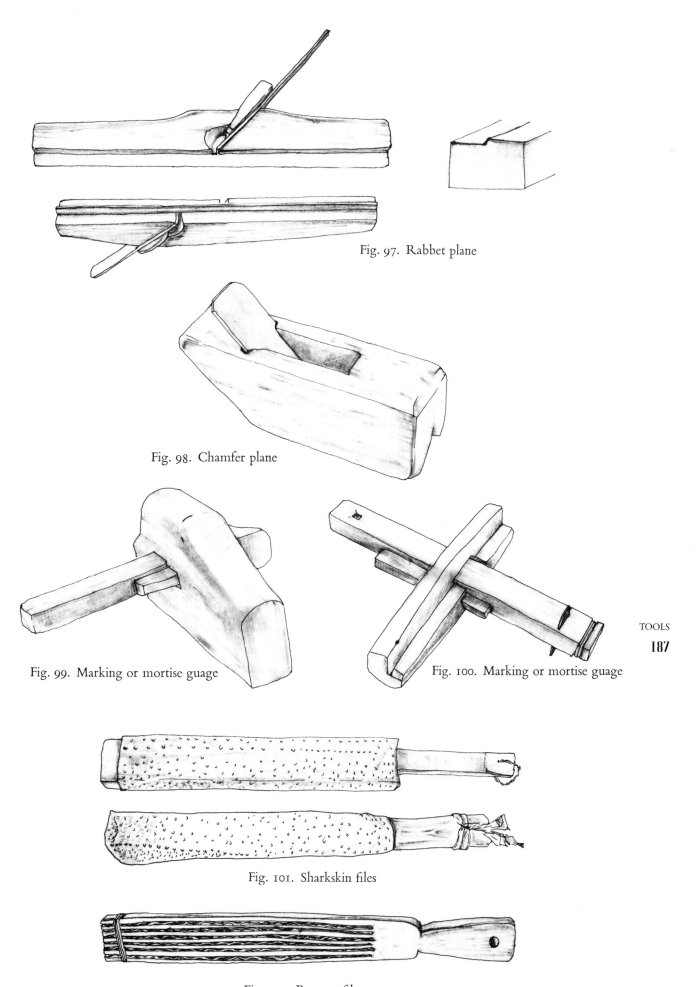

Fig. 97. Rabbet plane

Fig. 98. Chamfer plane

Fig. 99. Marking or mortise guage

Fig. 100. Marking or mortise guage

Fig. 101. Sharkskin files

Fig. 102. Rasp or file

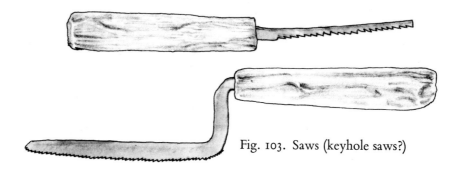
Fig. 103. Saws (keyhole saws?)

Fig. 104. Rattail file

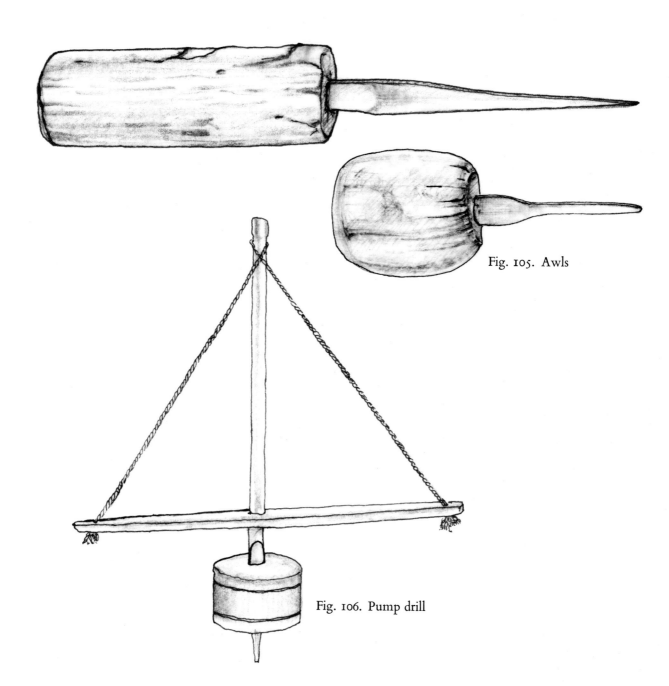

Fig. 105. Awls

Fig. 106. Pump drill

INDEX